STYLES OF URBAN POLICING

STYLES OF URBAN POLICING:
Organization, Environment, and Police Styles in Selected American Cities

Jeffrey S. Slovak

NEW YORK UNIVERSITY PRESS
New York *and* London

Library of Congress Cataloging-in-Publication Data

Slovak, Jeffrey S.
  Styles of urban policing.

  Bibliography: p.
  Includes index.
  1. Police—United States.   2. Police.
administration—United States.   I. Title.
HV8141.S59   1986   363.2'0973   86-5440
ISBN 0-8147-7855-0

Book design by Ken Venezio

Contents

Tables

Figures

Acknowledgments

Many people helped me in the production of this book and the research on which it is based, and I would like to acknowledge them here. My deepest thanks go to: Charles Hale and George Greisinger for first interesting me in the police; Koya Azumi, Robert Bursik, Clayton Hartjen, Albert Reiss, Lawrence Sherman, and Norman Washburne, for listening to, criticizing, and supporting my efforts; the Elyria, Columbia, and Newark Police Departments and their members; the National Science Foundation and the Rutgers University Research Council for invaluable financial support; Colin Jones and Despina P. Gimbel for their critical and editorial assistance; the many police officers who have taught me about their jobs and their lives; and Pat and Stephanie, who make it all worthwhile. The shortcomings of this book are wholly mine; its strengths owe much to my friends and colleagues.

STYLES OF URBAN POLICING

1. Organizations, Environments, and Styles in Urban Police Work

A casual traveler with an interest in police and their work cannot help but notice—and delight in—the contrasts among police officers in a variety of places. I am one such person, and I enjoyed this experience a few years ago, when I happened to travel to Acapulco, Mexico and Oxford, England within six months. In each place, I happened to observe a two-man, uniformed patrol working a regular daytime police beat; in neither case, did I see the officers involved take any formal police action. Other than their numbers and the fact that they wore uniforms, however, the two patrols I observed could not have had much less in common. The unarmed English "Bobbies" patrolled on bicycles and interacted readily and easily with the citizens and tourists they encountered; they seemed to enjoy the antics of the Oxford students, who were publicly and enthusiastically celebrating the end of their final examination period. The Bobbies' Mexican counterparts patrolled on foot, each partner carrying a 9-mm machine pistol and a holstered sidearm, and were much more reserved; they seemed uninterested in the antics of the tourists on the beach, and their interactions with citizens and strangers—which the policemen never initiated—were marked by a wary caution. I watched neither patrol deal with a crime or a dispute; nor did I see either initiate an investigation or intervene in a potentially disorderly situation. I have little doubt, however, that their styles would be quite different in this respect as well.

That police work as practiced by officers and experienced by citizens should vary widely from place to place is certainly not all that surprising. Take any two pairs of police officers, locate them in different countries (with different histories and traditions of policing), situate them in different environments which pose different problems of order and disorder, lodge them in different organizations replete with different missions, structures, and operating procedures, invest them with different working personalities, and leave them much freedom from direct supervision and hence much latitude in defining and carrying out their jobs, and the result is likely to be what James Q. Wilson has termed the "varieties of police behavior (1972)". Control the comparison somewhat by restricting the observations to one country or even one city, and the variety is no less, or only slightly less, likely.

This book is about some of the varieties of police work in the neighborhoods and precincts of urban America. Those varieties are many, and they manifest themselves not only among cities but also among the neighborhoods of any given city, as the writings of numerous students of American police so clearly demonstrate. Variations in police work are no less apparent in the specific cities and neighborhoods studied in what follows. This book takes an analytic approach to its subject and attempts to test alternative hypotheses about the factors that give rise to these observable varieties of policing. Its purpose is to uncover which of many competing variables best account for the variations in police action that are so readily apparent in American neighborhoods and cities. To paint with admittedly broad strokes, the varieties of interest here are the varying "styles" of police work experienced by residents in the neighborhoods of selected American cities; the analytic task the book undertakes is to determine whether these variations are more adequately explained by features of the neighborhoods in which police work or by aspects of the police organizations which employ them.

Neither the concept of a police style of working behavior nor the framing of an empirical study in terms of "organization versus environment" is new to sociology. The origins of the former date back nearly two decades to the research of James Q. Wilson (1972); the latter first became a serious issue in the study of business productivity and performance at approximately the same time, thanks to research by Paul Lawrence and Jay Lorsch (1967). What is distinctive about this book is the direct coupling of the two, the use of the latter as a perspective from which to gain a better understanding of variations in the former. To see how that is so, an extended word about both the concept and the perspective seems in order.

Styles of Urban Policing

In the late 1960s, James Q. Wilson developed an analysis of the work of American municipal police in a book (Wilson 1972) that has come to be considered a classic in the field. *Varieties of Police Behavior* was designed to portray in broad strokes the different ways police respond to the discretionary situations which they continually encounter in their daily rounds of activities. Toward that end, Wilson offered a general typology of police styles, distinguishing police departments by whether their approach to citizen encounters was service-oriented, legalistic, or watchmanlike. A few phrases from his narrative can serve as basic definitions for each of the three types.

In some communities, the police in dealing with situations that do not involve "serious" crime act as if order maintenance rather than law enforcement were their principal function. . . . The police are *watchman-like* not simply in emphasizing order over law enforcement but also in judging the seriousness of infractions less by what the law says about them than by their immediate and personal consequences, which will differ in importance depending on the standards of the relevant group. (1972:140)

In some departments . . . the officer is expected to take a *law enforcement* (legalistic) view of his role . . . to handle commonplace situations as if they were matters of law enforcement rather than order maintenance. . . . The police will act, on the whole, as if there were a single standard of community conduct—that which the law prescribes. (1972:172)

In some communities, the police take seriously all requests for either law enforcement or order maintenance . . . but are less likely to respond by making an arrest or imposing formal sanctions. . . . The police intervene frequently but not formally . . . [they] act as if their task were to estimate the "market" for police services and to produce a "product" that meets the demand. . . . Such a policy will be called the *"service"* style. (1972:200)

Wilson went on to offer empirical examples of each of these styles by describing the formal policies, organizational structures, and patrol activities in police agencies in eight urban or suburban communities in New York, Illinois, and California. In each and across all eight, he paid particular attention to the ways and means by which the nature of the community served and its local political system structured the demands of citizens for police service and the working styles predominant in the police agencies responding to those demands. That styles varied across his study sites and that at least some, and perhaps a great deal, of that variation could be attributed to different urban cultures and the attempts of police organizations to respond to them were the key messages that emerged from Wilson's analysis.

Varieties of Police Behavior was a special book: it addressed a substantive field (an institution and the people who operate it) which had previously been largely overlooked by social scientists; it exploded an implicit popular myth that guided thinking about that substantive field; and in doing both of these, it offered the prospect for building a science around the study of American police and police work. Little serious study of the police had previously been carried out by scholars, and much of that work (see primarily Westley 1953, 1956) suggested that American policing was necessarily and sufficiently secretive in nature to preclude the doing of much more. *Varieties of Police Behavior* mapped a path through virtually virgin terrain, and it did so with such care and detail as to dispel at least some of the secrecy. Further, it exploded the myth that police everywhere were pretty much alike and carried out common functions in the communities they served. The variations that Wilson uncovered with regard to style were more in kind than in degree; his eight study sites housed police agencies pursuing demonstrably different missions. Amid the variation, however, was some system. Wilson did not merely report on eight discrete case studies, but rather ordered his results to support a scholarly, propositional argument on the sources of the variations he uncovered. *Varieties of Police Behavior* exploded a myth of police homogeneity and replaced it, not with another myth of random variation, but with a scientific causal hypothesis that virtually demanded further research and testing.

The years since the first publication of *Varieties of Police Behavior* have witnessed an explosion of police research.[1] Trained observers have ridden or walked countless details and shifts with working police officers, recording and analyzing the ways they make decisions about law, order, and justice and the ways they pursue all three (Skolnick 1967); the types of situations that lead them to employ violence (Rubinstein 1973; the entire issue of the *Annals of the American Academy of Political and Social Science* for November 1980); and the ways they justify the actions they take (Manning 1978a; Ericson 1982). Surveys and questionnaires have been developed and administered to police officers to measure their levels of cynicism (Niederhoffer

1969), attitudes toward minorities (Bayley and Mendelsohn 1969), degrees of job satisfaction (Slovak 1978) and levels of commitment to and enthusiasm about their jobs (Van Maanen 1975). Analyses of census data have uncovered the connections between police manpower allocations and budget expenditures and a variety of urban political and social characteristics (Jacobs 1979; Liska, Lawrence, and Benson 1981; Jackson and Carroll 1981; Liska and Chamlin 1984). Histories of individual police departments have been written (Lane 1967; Richardson 1970; Fogelson 1977). Experiments and quasi-experiments have been developed to assess the efficacy of different types of police operation (Kelling et al. 1974; Sherman et al. 1973; Sherman and Berk 1984) and special studies have focused on discrete, unique groups of police officers: blacks (Alex 1969; Leinen 1984), women (Milton 1972; Martin 1980), those working on urban skid rows (Bittner 1967), detectives (Skolnick 1967) and new recruits to police work (Harris 1973), to name only a few. In addition, a body of literature describing and comparing police functions and practices in and across different nations (Banton 1964; Bayley 1969, 1976; Ames 1981; Williams 1979; Liang 1970) has arisen as well. It would be unfair and inaccurate, of course, to argue that this explosion of police research was attributable completely to the publication of *Varieties of Police Behavior*. External events that occurred at roughly the same—the urban disorders of the late 1960s in American cities and the charges of police insensitivity and brutality that accompanied them, the involvement of the U.S. Law Enforcement Assistance Administration in promoting and underwriting research on police, the exposure of notorious instances of police corruption—were much stronger directing forces in this regard. Even so, however, *Varieties of Police Behavior* stood through it all as a work that could guide the efforts of scientists propelled by these external events to study the American police. It quickly became and remains one of the most frequently cited books in its field.

For all of the citations, however, and for all that we have learned from the police research explosion, there is a very real sense in which the promise offered by Wilson's original analysis has gone unfulfilled. A glance back at the topics listed above that have received scholarly attention turns up an interesting anomaly: virtually none of the studies noted deals explicitly with the style of police service. The body of citations is admittedly an incomplete one and some of the topics that its entries address are arguably related to style, yet the impression it creates is essentially correct. Few scholars besides Wilson himself (Wilson and Boland 1978) have made use of the concept of style in their work, and most of those that have (most notably Muir 1977 and Brown 1981) have used it as a characteristic of individual police officers and not of police organizations. With a very few exceptions (Talarico and Swanson 1978; Ferdinand 1976), style has not appeared in the literature as a characteristic of an aggregate of police, be it one based on a precinct, a departmental unit, or an entire organization. As a result, much that Wilson suggested about variations in police style remains tentative, unconfirmed by subsequent efforts conducted in settings and among officers different from those he originally studied.

In part, the culprit here is Wilson himself. His definitions of the service, watchman, and legalistic styles, certainly have a ring of realism to them; the differences in police action to which they point are differences that many of us encounter if we are at all attentive to the nature of police work in the various places where we live, work, and travel. From a scientific perspective, however, those definitions pose something of a problem. How precisely do we categorize any given police department as having a predominant orientation toward any one of the three styles? How do we identify mixed cases? What observations must we make in order to classify a police agency as service-oriented, watchmanlike, or legalistic? Wilson himself is straightforward about the classifications he makes of his eight study cases, but much less so about the bases he employs for making those classifications. When he operationalizes the styles at all, he appears to place much weight on the degree to which local police are aggressive in enforcing traffic ordinances (Wilson and Boland 1978)—an interesting variable for some purposes, but a radical simplification of a concept as multidimensional as police style. For a study breaking new ground in a field, some imprecision may be acceptable. Researchers seeking to replicate and extend that research, however, face a serious problem; they must develop their own empirical indicators with little guidance from the seminal treatment of the topic. That few have done so with regard to police style is thus, in part, attributable to that seminal imprecision.

Another part of the reason for the relative abandonment of police style as a research variable is undoubtedly its generality. Wilson's narrative treatment makes it abundantly clear that he intends his typology to cover virtually everything that the police in any given community do—at least everything they do to and for the local citizenry. The typology itself is an ideal-typical construction, much like Max Weber's classic treatment of bureaucracy (1922); individual police departments are expected to approach but never to perfectly embody one or the other of the analytically pure types. Yet we observers are expected to classify them on the basis of all their actions: how they deal with traffic infractions, drunks, middle-class citizens, blacks, juveniles, prostitutes, and drug users, to name only those that figure prominently in Wilson's narrative. To capture all of this in one variable or under one categorical label is a formidable task, one that in some ways runs counter to the analytical, dissecting specificity that characterizes much of science. Perhaps it is little wonder that subsequent scholars of American police began to focus on the parts, or what they inferred from Wilson's narrative as the parts, rather than the whole of the concept of police style.

Because it focuses on police style as the phenomenon for variations in which an explanation is to be sought, and because it does so by means of a methodology that attempts to operationalize style in a manner true to Wilson's original definitions, this book has a flavor of the "old" about it. Much current research on policing is based on a deterrence model; it seeks to uncover the extent to which police officers and police actions, and especially arrests, have demonstrable effects on rates of crime and/or violence in the settings where those officers and actions are observed (Kelling et al. 1974; Sherman and Berk 1984; Loftin and McDowall 1982). That question goes unasked in this book, so that the focus can center on its logically prior counterpart: what gives rise to the varieties of police action? For all their ambiguities, Wilson's original definitions of the three police styles recognize that crime-fighting and criminal apprehension constitute only one facet—and in terms of the time police actually spend at it, a fairly small facet—of the totality of police work. To focus on that totality, as embodied in the idea of police style, is to focus on the real multidimensionality of the phenomenon of interest. To do so is also to make possible the methodological refinement and replication required to assess the scientific worth of the concept of police style. Finally, to do so is to raise and to answer a question which neither Wilson nor most subsequent scholars have seriously explored—that of the relative strengths of organization as opposed to environment in generating and structuring police action.

Organization Versus Environment

The link between a formal organization and its operating environment has become a critical topic for research. Some years ago, Paul Lawrence and Jay Lorsch (1967) demonstrated that business productivity, innovation, and growth were contingent on the fit between a company's internal structure and its external markets for labor, raw materials, and finished products. Since then, others (most notably Pfeffer and Salancik 1978) have demonstrated that many of the structural and functional facets of an organization are critically subject to "external countrol," while organizational ecologists (Freeman and Hannan 1983; Hannan and Freeman 1984) have noted that pure organizational survival is contingent on the character of the environmental niche the organization occupies. It would seem today a matter of general agreement that we cannot fully understand any organization, or the character and quality of the product it produces, without understanding the transactions in which it engages with the world outside its boundaries.

The focus on organization–environment ties and on their ramifications for organizational outputs is arguably even more critical in the study of the police than it is in that of other types of organizations. As Albert Reiss and David Bordua (1967) have argued,

All organizations can be so studied, of course, but . . . the police have as their fundamental task the creation and maintenance of, and their participation in, external relationships. Indeed, the central meaning of police authority itself is its significance as a mechanism for "managing" relationships. (1967:25–26)

Despite their suggestion, however, and the proliferation of empirical studies of police since they made it, there is an important sense in which most police research has neglected to focus on organization–community interchanges, and especially on the differential impacts of each partner in the pairing on local police service. By far, the largest component of the environment of a police agency is the citizenry that it serves, and studies of police–citizen interactions abound. The best of them (Black 1970; Black and Reiss 1970; Piliavin and Briar 1964; Sykes and Brent 1983; Sykes and Clark 1975) show that police action is significantly determined by citizen demand and demeanor. From such findings, some scholars have argued that police work in general is situationally determined (Manning 1977). The primary problem with most such formulations and the research based on them is that they neglect organization altogether. As Punch (1983) and others have noted, most of the outstanding studies of police–citizen encounters have not been interorganizational in terms of their designs but rather intraorganizational; most have been conducted in a single agency or setting,[2] and most have focused on individual police officers as their units of analysis. The attitudes and actions of those individual officers and the way they are shaped by citizen encounters become the focus of attention, and the larger police organization that conditions those same attitudes and actions is largely ignored. In light of the recent studies conducted by Muir (1977) and Brown (1981), each of which amasses evidence from different police agencies of the importance of managerial and supervisory styles in structuring police officers' actions in and perspectives on their work, this omission is clearly problematic, and its implications are broad.

Recent scholarship has focused more directly than ever on the nature, structure, and performance of the corporate actor—the formal organization with goals and strategies which are uniquely its own and not, or at least not necessarily, simply the aggregated interests of its members. James Coleman (1974, 1982) has demonstrated rather clearly how the goals of corporate actors regularly diverge from those of their individual members as well as the general population of individuals they serve. This divergence is rooted in the very nature of organization itself. With regard to the police, Bordua and Reiss (1966) have alerted us to the way connections between the police executive and the local political hierarchy ramify throughout the police organization; further, Gerald Caiden (1977) and Michael Brown (1981), among others, have argued that the wave of professionalization so widely heralded by and among American police in the period since the disorders of the late 1960s was a peculiarly organizational phenomenon. It focused specifically on centralization of executive authority and enhancement of central control over the exercise of street-level discretion. All of this points to the police organization as a critical actor in its own right. It suggests that police departments and the officers they house are a good deal more than simple reactors to the expectations of citizens and the pressures of politicians. To the contrary, they actively choose their missions, and design strategies to meet them; and they tailor those strategies to the different settings in which they are enacted.

Such a picture of police organizations throws a whole new cast on questions of both theory and policy. With regard to the former, consider the definition of the process of social control offered recently by Gibbs: "an attempt by one party to manipulate the behavior of another party through still another party by any means other than a chain of command." (1982:86) To most social theorists and researchers, police are one of the quintessential agents of formal social control operating in the local community. They act at the behest of the law and its dictates and at the behest of those groups who control the local political and legislative structures to "manipulate" the actions of those who would threaten the social order. They stand in the middle of a simple chain model that links intentionality of the controllers to the response of their agents to the actions or nonactions of the controlled. If the police themselves, however, are proactive and police agencies are the rational corporate actors of Coleman, Caiden, or Brown, then this model immediately becomes problematic. At the very least, intentionality is shared across the first two links in the social control chain; at the most, it is monopolized by the second. The "real" functions of the police, their connections to the local power elite, and the processes of achieving internal control of police organizations become central issues in police research, and the elimination or subversion of representative decisionmaking in the area of law enforcement arises as an issue for members of the community and political theorists alike.

Questions of police policy and planning also take on a different cast if the police organization is anything like that depicted above. Policy evaluation in police research has focused rather heavily on three topics: police effectiveness in generating arrests and lowering crime rates (Votey and Phillips 1972; Wilson and Boland 1978; Jacob and Rich 1981; Parks and Ostrom 1981; Loftin and McDowall 1982; Kelling et al. 1974; Sherman and Berk 1984; Berk and Newton 1985), police efficiency per resource expended (Ostrom et al. 1973; Skogan, 1976) and citizen satisfaction with police action and demeanor (Aberbach and Walker 1970; Ostrom et al. 1971; Phillips and Politzer 1982). All three of these dimensions of policy evaluation erect what is essentially an external standard against which to measure police action, although scholars working with each usually presume it to be an internal standard for police departments as well. Police agencies that wholly or partially choose their own missions make problematic both this presumption and the general evaluative utility of the external standards. Instead, they throw us back on logically prior questions. How are the goals and missions of police agencies generated? What are the organizational dynamics behind both the adoption and the subversion of innovative police procedures and practices? How do police agencies maintain their freedom of action in the face of citizens' expectations and political elites' demands? As our picture of the contemporary police department comes more into line with corporate actor theory, questions like these grow in importance while the salience of the more standard evaluative inquiries recedes.

There are other implications and issues that might be detailed here, but those listed are sufficient to make the basic point. Even with the wealth of research that has been conducted on and about police officers and the citizens they touch, we know comparatively little about police organizations, and even less about the differential effects of organizations and environments on the styles of local police work produced for and experienced by a local community. To probe those in some detail is the key analytic task this book undertakes. In this sense, too, the book takes up an "old" topic, for Wilson originally posited police style as an organizational and not an individual phenomenon. We do not automatically make the same assumption here. While the style of police work is indeed treated in what follows at an aggregate rather than an individual level, the degree to which style is generated organizationally, environmentally, or by some combination of both is left open as the central issue for empirical analysis and verification.

Plan of the Book

In light of its focus on a "new" or at least generally unexamined question about police work using an "old" but generally undeveloped dependent variable, this book of necessity has both a substantive and a methodological goal. The former, that of pitting organization against environment as causal agents in the production of police styles and determining the roles of each in that regard, is primary. Implicit in it and necessary to its attainment is the latter goal, that of developing methodologically precise and valid definitions and reliable and replicatable operationalizations of the type of police style. Throughout the narrative, however, we focus on street-level police styles not as functions of the attitudes and actions of individual working officers but rather as functions of the cities and neighborhoods in which they are enacted and of the agencies whose members do the enacting.

Chapter 2 offers a substantive introduction to the "organization versus environment" analytical issue in the study of policing. In terms of the number of cases with which it deals and the number of variables it seeks to analyze, it is arguably the broadest chapter in the book. What it gains in breadth, however, it sacrifices in depth. In it, a secondary analysis of data on a sample of 42 sizable American cities is offered. Characteristics of the cities' environments and of the structures of their police organizations are used to predict their arrest rates for the two major types of serious criminal offenses. The arrest rates are arguably a component of police style, especially of the legalistic variety, although they are clearly not equivalent to it; here, obviously, is where the sacrifice of depth is encountered. The results of this exercise, when compared with the findings offered by other students of urban arrest rates, rather clearly document the importance of organizational factors in structuring police action. They also suggest a series of detailed hypotheses about the determinants of legalistic policing that are amenable to further research. The unsatisfactory nature of arrest rates as measures of police styles, however, motivates the search for stronger measures and alternative research designs and study settings in which the same substantive issue and the specific hypotheses yielded by this empirical analysis can be addressed.

The remaining chapters take up this pursuit of a more satisfactory study of urban police styles. Taken together, they seek to argue for and demonstrate the utility of data captured in police dispatch logs for the analysis of street-level police styles; to develop operationalizations of police styles that are both amenable to empirical research and replicable analysis, and at the same time are substantively true to Wilson's original definitions; and to apply those measures in a further test of the differential effects of organization and environment in generating local police styles.

The data on which these chapters are based measure the styles of police work experienced by each of 50 urban neighborhoods or environments, distributed across three different American cities that are served by three different municipal police departments. Using such data puts us in a position to analyze variations in police style among the neighborhoods of each of the three cities considered separately, and across the entire collection as well, in the search for the differential effects of policing environment and police organization on the delivery of a particular style of police work.

The remainder of the book is divided into five chapters. The three cities to be studied in depth vary considerably from each other, but nevertheless are in no technical sense of the term a "sample." Hence, it is important to identify as precisely as possible how they differ from each other and from other cities, and how those differences in turn might affect the conduct of local police work. That is the task of chapter 3. Chapter 4 is both methodological and substantive in tone. It examines, first in a general way, the kinds of data on police action available to a researcher from a police dispatch log, focusing particularly on the strengths and weaknesses of using such material for the analytical purposes of a study like this one. It then examines the particular information recording processes upon which the police dispatch logs in the three research sites are constructed, and displays results on the availability and quality of the data they they yield. From this examination emerges another prospective hypothesis about the relation between police organizations' information systems and their styles, a hypothesis to be further examined as empirical results emerge. Chapter 4 then offers detailed descriptions of the variations in police work that the dispatch log data yield in each of the three study sites. Serial analyses of the data from each city are offered here because not all the measures with which we might ideally work are uniformly available for all three subject police agencies. Separate analyses offer a detailed feel for police work in each site, while they make maximum use of the available data. Nonetheless, the chapter is not solely or simply descriptive; at its conclusion, it specifically addresses empirical commonalities to attempt to identify what is common to urban police work and what is unique to the individual police department.

Chapter 5 combines substance and method. First, it focuses explicitly on the concept of a police style to derive a set of empirical indicators of the two most salient dimensions of that concept: the rate of police aggressiveness in a given neighborhood, and the degree to which substantive local police work is legalistic, watchmanlike, or service-oriented. These measures are then used in an analysis of style variations across both neighborhoods and cities. The results of that exercise are juxtaposed with the empirical expectations derived from the hypotheses constructed in earlier chapters and from Michael Brown's (1981) hypothesis on the size of the department and the discretion of the officer. The "tests" of these hypotheses offered in chapter 5 lend much support to the argument for organizational determination of local policing styles, and comparatively little to its environmental counterpart.

In Chapter 6, the organization–environment question is put to its most rigorous empirical test, using the data from the three cities of interest. From available census data, measures are constructed of the social, demographic, and economic characteristics of each of the neighborhoods. Those aspects of the local environment of police work are then matched against city-level differences in a series of two- and three-way analyses of variance and multiple classification analyses of the dimensions of police style (as defined and presented in chapter 5). What emerges here is the substantial importance of organization at the expense of environment in structuring patterns of local police action.

Chapter 7 concludes the book. It uses a brief review of what has gone before to launch into a discussion of issues that might guide future efforts in the empirical study of the police. Some of those address theoretical aspects of social control in modern society, and some address the more policy-relevant domains of police practice and management; but all focus on the importance of the police organization as a corporate actor in the social life of the local urban community.

Notes

1. As one indicator, note that in 1972 what had for many years been the *Journal of Criminal Law, Criminology and Police Science* became two separate journals: the *Journal of Criminal Law and Criminology* and the *Journal of Police Science and Administration*.
2. There are some exceptions to this, most recently the detailed analysis across three police departments and four work settings offered by Michael Brown (1981). This is an important work, which is addressed in some detail below. For now, it is sufficient to note that it *is* an exception.

2. Legalistic Policing in Urban America: A City-Level Perspective

In their recent study "Crime Control in American Cities," sociologists Allen Liska and Mitchell Chamlin (1984) offer a theoretically tight and empirically convincing demonstration of the way urban arrest rates are structured by the social and particularly the racial contours of the cities in which they are registered. Liska and Chamlin ground their study in an approach generally known as conflict theory, a perspective that views arrests as a form of social control levied upon the powerless by the agents of influential elites seeking to maintain their privileged positions. That perspective, in fact, guides most empirical research on police resource allocations and criminal apprehensions. The approach is not without its critics (Beirne 1979), but its successes in explaining variations in the phenomena to which it has been applied are many, as are its scholarly adherents.

Like most conflict theorists, Liska and Chamlin do not in their research specifically address the question of whether police organizational dynamics have anything unique to do with the generation of arrest rates. This is by no means a personal shortcoming or fault of theirs. Traditional conflict theory relegates such a question to the status of the trivial, by assuming that the proximate agents of social control are indeed *agents* of the lawmakers and power-wielders. If the work of controlling carried out by those agents is indeed completely determined by the will of the elite as that is in turn shaped by the character of the community setting, then omitting any treatment of the structure of the agents' organization is neither a theoretical oversight nor an empirical misspecification (Blalock 1982). Rather, it is a sensible research strategy, given the assumptions underlying the theoretical perspective.

From the successes that conflict theory has compiled in explaining urban police departments' manpower allocations, budget expenditures, and operations, it would seem that the burden of proof would now lie with the plaintiff, should he or she argue for the independent importance of police organizational dynamics in this same regard. The purpose of this chapter is to begin to take up that burden of proof. It follows the lead of Liska and Chamlin, and of other conflict theorists as well, by focusing on arrest rates across a sample of American cities and by seeking to explain variations in those. It departs from that lead by treating the organizational dimensions of urban policing not as trivial but rather as theoretically important and empirically problematic. In short, it seeks to pose and answer the question of whether organizational and environmental factors have unique differential effects on arrest rates in American urban areas.

Few who have studied urban arrest rates have treated them as indicators of police working styles. Nonetheless, that is our intention here. Clearly, police arrest rates are not equivalent to police styles; as we have already noted, the latter are too multidimensional to be captured completely, or even adequately, by the former alone. It is arguable, however, that arrest rates are reasonable indicators of the styles, capable of tapping at least the major behavioral distinctions between aggressive legalistic policing in one community and its more reactive, watchmanlike counterpart in another. Our analysis proceeds on that assumption. In doing so, it offers an introductory treatment of the organization versus environment issue as it is played out in American urban policing and especially in the generation of its legalistic varieties.

Cases, Data Sources, and Measures

The focal units of analysis in this chapter are the 42 American cities and their police departments studied between 1976 and 1979 by Public Administration Service (PAS), a not-for-profit research and consulting firm headquartered in McLean, Virginia. The PAS study was underwritten by the National Institute of Law Enforcement and Criminal Justice. The 42 cities are those that agreed to participate in the study, from among the 51 cities of the National Opinion Research Center's Permanent Community Sample (Rossi and Crain 1968), studied extensively by Terry Clark and his colleagues (Clark 1968; Clark and Ferguson 1983). The Permanent Community Sample was initially selected as a stratified probability sample of the places of residence of the American urban population; the 42 cities that participated in the PAS study proved, after extensive testing on key variables (Greisinger, Slovak, and Molkup 1979), to be an unbiased sample of Clark's 51. Accordingly, an analysis of them should offer a reasonably reliable introductory portrait of the nature and determinants of legalistic policing in American cities.

Data on the social and demographic characteristics of American cities are plentiful and readily available thanks to the U.S. Census, while FBI files contain arrest rates for a host of cities. Data on the structural characteristics of American police departments, unfortunately, are few and far between. The advantage in using the 42 cases and some of the data compiled on them by the PAS study, which was heavily organizational in focus, is that the latter fill in this gap rather well. In any event, the data used here are of three general types and come from three separate sources. Those that measure urban characteristics come generally from the 1970 Census; the only exceptions are a pair of measures of city political structures, which were originally compiled by Clark (1968). Data on arrests come from FBI files for calendar year 1976. Data on the police agency characteristics come from formal, structured interviews conducted with police officials in each of the 42 police agencies, as part of the original PAS study. These data, too, tap the policing situation in each study site as of 1976.

Urban Characteristics. The empirical literature on police strength (Jacobs 1979; Liska, Lawrence, and Benson 1981; Loftin, Kessler, and Greenberg 1984), police spending (Jackson and Carroll 1981) and arrest rates (Wilson and Boland 1978; Jacob and Rich 1981; Liska and Chamlin 1984) suggests a plethora of urban characteristics that are to some degree associated with each of these aspects of urban policing. The results of these studies in part guided the selection of variables used in this analysis to tap the general nature of the urban environment in which police work is carried out. In addition, variable selection was guided by the tradition of research in urban ecology which has uncovered a consistent set of basic dimensions by which American cities can be differentiated and classified (Berry 1972; Rees 1972;

Berry and Kasarda 1977). Because there are relatively few units of analysis for this exercise, the analytic procedure followed here is to compile data on a range of city characteristics, subject those to a factor analysis, and use scores on the general dimensions of urbanization yielded by this procedure to measure variations in city environments.

Fifteen specific measures of city characteristics were tapped for the initial factor analysis: city size; reported violent and property crime rates per 10,000 residents; region (a dummy variable distinguishing southern from nonsouthern cities); percentages of the city population that are children (age 5 or younger), teenagers (age 10 to 19), married, black, and of foreign stock; the percent of females employed outside the home; the percent of households with incomes at or above $10,000; the percent of owner-occupied housing; median years of completed schooling; median home values; and average household densities. The factor analytic procedure applied to these variables—a principal components analysis with oblique factor rotation—generated a four-factor solution which explains 77.4 percent of the common variance of the fifteen measures. The factor structure matrix, the communalities of specific variables with these factors, and the interfactor correlations are displayed in table 2.1. The strongest factor loading associated with each specific variable is also highlighted in the table.

The four dimensions of differentiation yielded by this procedure and their specific variable components are generally congruent with the results generated by other studies using similar procedures. The first factor can be labeled a dimension of "familism," linking as it does high marriage proportions, household density and owner-occupancy levels and percentages of children and teens. The second factor can be labeled "regional poverty," and links southern location of a city (and, peripherally, a larger black community) with lower incomes and home values and relatively few persons of foreign stock. The third factor is a reasonably straightforward "socioeconomic status" dimension, linking high levels of educational attainment, high home values, and large proportions of women working outside the home. Finally, the fourth factor is labeled "urbanization," and links large populations, high rates of reported violent and property crime, and relatively large black communities.

As indicated in table 2.1, the correlations among these general dimensions of differentiation are relatively mild. More urbanized cities

Table 2.1. Dimensions of Differentiation in 42 American Cities

| | Factor Structure Loadings | | | | |
Variables	Factor 1 (Familism)	Factor 2 (Regional Poverty)	Factor 3 (Socio-Economic Status)	Factor 4 (Urban-ization)	Communality
% Teenagers	.877	.364	-.164	-.191	.811
Household Density	.962	.118	-.200	-.192	.943
% Children	.826	.168	-.276	-.001	.753
% Owner-Occupied Housing	.775	.283	.007	-.528	.788
Median Schooling	-.120	-.052	.847	-.215	.761
Median Home Value	-.285	-.704	.722	-.095	.882
% High Incomes	.278	-.655	.590	-.498	.915
% Black	-.314	.579	-.253	.691	.767
% Foreign Stock	-.449	-.864	.046	-.207	.866
Violent Crime Rate	-.346	.211	-.149	.965	.949
Property Crime Rate	-.165	.260	.252	.622	.515
City Size (Population)	-.012	.195	-.190	.658	.469
% Women Working Outside Residence	-.275	-.140	.407	.163	.244
% Married Adults	.515	.161	-.050	-.206	.280
Southern Location	.227	.805	-.108	.171	.657

Inter-Factor Correlations

	F_1	F_2	F_3	F_4
F_1	1.0	—	—	—
F_2	.187	1.0	—	—
F_3	-.126	-.172	1.0	—
F_4	-.251	.216	-.090	1.0

Note: The strongest loadings of specific variables on the factors produced for this analysis are highlighted with italics.

tend to be slightly less familistic ($r = -.25$) and a bit more likely to be poor, black and southern ($r = .22$), but these tendencies are relatively slight. The other coefficients in the bottom panel of table 2.1 are too low to merit sustained discussion.

There is now a large social scientific literature to support the contention that, in general, community political structures are critical intervening links between urban characteristics and public sector policy and program outputs. (For a bibliographic sampling of this literature, see Clark 1973.) In the specific area of police programs and outputs, relatively few scholars have probed the nature of this connection in empirical research; nonetheless, most would agree that the matter is worth pursuing. For purposes of this analysis, two measures of local political structure were included among the data for each of the 42 cities: (1) a dichotomous variable distinguishing cities administered by an elected mayor from those run by an appointed city manager, and (2) the index of political decentralization of the local decision making structure originally developed and calculated by Clark (1968). Both measures played key roles in Clark and Ferguson's (1983) analysis of city spending patterns and levels of fiscal strain while, in the context of policing, the former is central as a proposed causal variable in the discussion of "professional policing" which, as Bordua and Reiss (1966) describe it, sounds generally similar to legalistic policing.

Figure 2.1 summarizes and displays in path model form the links between and among these characteristics of the urban environments in which police work is carried out. The values of R^2 offered there suggest that the model is reasonably successful in explaining the aspects of the urban polity that it analyzes. In light of other studies of governmental form (Schnore and Alford 1963; Hawley 1975; Knoke 1982) and community decentralization (Clark 1968), there are no real surprises here. The key results of this exercise are that: the manager-council form of government is much more likely to occur in high-than in low-status cities; more urbanized communities have more decentralized political decision making systems; and the manager-council form of government tends to generate more centralized community decision making systems.

In any event, these findings will stand as the basic environmental template upon which the arrest-rate indicators of police legalism will be superimposed.

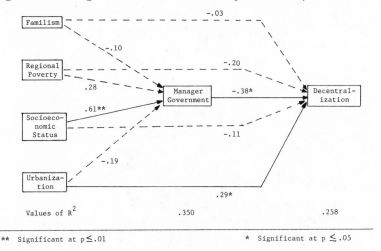

Values of R² = .350 ... .258

** Significant at p ≤ .01   * Significant at p ≤ .05

Figure 2.1. The Structure of the Social and Political Environment of Policing

Organization Characteristics. If the body of literature on community structures and characteristics can fairly be considered large (and it can), then that on formal organizations can only be termed mammoth. From the studies in that field that focus on the structuring of organizations, however, a general model has emerged which appears to command a reasonable consensus among empirical researchers. That model, depicted schematically in figure 2.2, can be summarized in a small set of basic proposition: larger organizations are more heavily differentiated in the work tasks they encompass; larger organizations require less intensive internal administration by virtue of the economies of scale they can enjoy, but more differentiated organizations (which also tend to be large) require more intensive administration to coordinate the various tasks they do; and the adoption of innovations by organizations is promoted by high levels of internal differentiation, but is discouraged by large size and by administrative intensity.

As might be expected, the degree to which each of these propositions holds varies somewhat from study to study, but their general validity seems well established. (See Hage 1980 for a summary of the literature in the field.)

While none of the major empirical efforts that contributed to the development of this general model were directed at urban police departments, a number were conducted among other kinds of public

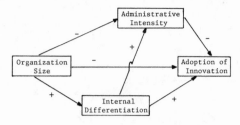

Figure 2.2. Conceptual Model of Organizational Structure

sector service agencies (Blau and Schoenherr 1971; Blau 1972). In that the latter, like police departments, typically provide services that are heavily labor-intensive, are generally not responsive to market signals, and must compete with other organizations in political budgetmaking contests for their input resources, a model that describes their structuring is a reasonable standard against which to compare data and findings on the previously unstudied police departments. Accordingly, that model generally guides the organizational analyses that follow.

For purposes of this exercise, the four aspects of organizational structure depicted in figure 2.2 were operationalized for the 42 police departments of interest here in the following ways:

Organization Size: Number of full-time police employees (sworn or civilian)
Division of Labor: Percent of sworn officers assigned to patrol duty
Administrative Intensity: Number of patrol officers per police sergeant
Innovation$_1$: Percent of employees who are civilians (civilianization)
Innovation$_2$: Percent of sworn officers who are black

The second and third are, of course, inverse measures; for each, lower scores index higher levels of the concepts of interest. Further, a skewed initial distribution of the third led to its logarithm being substituted into the actual statistical computations.

Because the innovations analyzed here concern manpower complements rather than technology or field practices, one change is required in the expectations embodied in the general heuristic model of organizational structures that guides this effort. The proposition that size constrains the adoption of the latter types of innovations is indeed fairly well established in the literature. So, however, is the proposition that large collectivities contain a greater diversity of members than do their smaller counterparts. Civilianization and aggressive recruitment and deployment of black police officers were innovations for American police agencies in the late 1960s and into the 1970s, (Leinen 1984) but, in light of their character as diversity-generating innovations, it seems more reasonable to expect more (rather than less) of both in larger (rather than smaller) police agencies.

Figure 2.3 summarizes in path model form the relationships between and among these indicators of the salient dimensions of police organizational structure. The values of R^2 offered there are generally disappointing but that is probably due in part to the "artificiality" of applying this model in the police context, where selected structural characteristics may well be affected by environmental and especially political forces. That is only to be expected for an agency whose resources are allocated in public-sector budgetmaking processes. To the extent that this problem of model misspecification is a serious one, the specific coefficients reported in figure 2.3 are equally artificial (Blalock 1982). Thus, rather than focusing unduly on these results, it seems sufficient simply to note that among the police departments studied here it would for the moment appear that: organizational size has no discernible effect on internal police agency differentiation; administrative intensity is a negative function of organizational size (recall that span of control, as measured here, is an inverse indicator of intensity) but is not directly related to differentiation; the innovation of civilianization is promoted by administrative intensity (again, recall that caveat about measurement) but is not directly affected by either size or differentiation; while, a large black police presence is promoted by organizational size but is not directly affected by either internal differentiation or administrative intensity.

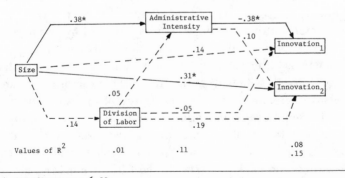

* Significant at p < .05

Figure 2.3. The Structure of the Police Organization

Many of these observed findings are consistent with the expectations for them contained in the general model of organizational structures. That impression is further reinforced if we look only to the signs of the coefficients displayed in figure 2.3, in which case consistencies appear twice as often as inconsistencies. Even so, the caveat about artificiality due to model misspecification, as noted above, remains well taken here and motivates further empirical investigation.

The Production of Arrest Rates

A police officer who makes an arrest is engaging in a discretionary act; while all officers are sworn to fully enforce all laws in the jurisdictions they serve, full enforcement is a practical impossibility (Davis 1975). Even when the arrest is made for what is consensually recognized as a serious crime, the act is no less discretionary (LaFave 1965); police are well known to define "serious" in somewhat different ways for the different subpopulations they serve.

To make an arrest is, of course, to impose a legal definition on and to deliver a legal solution to a social problem. It is to police "legalistically," in terms of Wilson's (1972) policing styles. Aggregated across all the police officers serving a jurisdiction, the total arrest rate stands as an approximate indicator of the degree to which the police department adopts a legalistic organizational style and provides its services accordingly.

From what sources does this choice of styles spring? Is it determined situationally by the responses of police officers—individually and in the aggregate—to the settings they police and the problems of order inherent in those settings? Is it determined by organizational policies, procedures, and structural arrangements; and if so, are the latter functions of setting as well? These are not rhetorical questions; to the contrary, they embody at the city level of analysis the organization versus environment debate in the context of legalistic police work.

As a first approach to answering these queries, figure 2.4 displays and compares the results of four path-analytic statistical modeling exercises. Two of the four examine the determinants of arrest rates for violent crimes, defined here (and by the FBI) as murder, rape, robbery, and assault; the other two focus on arrest rates for property crimes, defined as burglary, grand larceny, and auto theft. Arrest rates for the latter group probably approach a purer indicator of the legalistic police style, in that the discretion to make the arrests is broader; it is hard to imagine public opinion becoming quite so inflamed over low larceny arrest rates as it would undoubtedly be over equally low murder arrest rates. Nonetheless, the former include discretionary situations as well, and are worth examining here. The four models are further distinguished; two are intended as "pure" environmental models that deliberately exclude organizational determinants of police legalism, while the other two stand as "pure" organizational models that exclude environmental determinants. The caveats noted earlier about model misspecification are equally relevant here, especially for the pure organizational models; the comparison intended by the models displayed in figure 2.4 is and must be a heuristic, proximate one.

The first thing to note about the models is that all four do creditable to excellent jobs of explaining the variance in their respective dependent variables, with values of R^2 ranging from .39 to .76. The models of arrest rates for violent crimes outperform those for property crimes in this regard, a fact consistent with our earlier speculation about the differential amounts of discretion reflected in the arrest situations for each. Nonetheless, all four models capture substantively notable dynamics in the arrest phenomena that they examine.

A second point worth noting about these models is the consistency across arrest types of the directions of causal effects that they reveal. Magnitudes of effects vary, but if we disregard this for a moment and focus only on the directions of those effects we see that in the "pure" environmental models, four of the six direct paths to the dependent variable are consistently positive or consistently negative, while in the "pure" organizational models, all five direct effects maintain this consistency of direction. The types of police legalism captured in these different arrest rates are not equivalent, but the differences seem from these results to be matters more of degree than of kind.

A quick glance at figure 2.4 establishes that the pure environmental model outperforms its organizational counterpart for both kinds of arrest rates; differences here, however, are in general less than remarkable. That fact suggests—although it does not demonstrate—that both capture important causal dynamics in the production of police legalism.

While the models in figure 2.4 suggest that the levels of civilianizations and minority presence in a police department and the degree of

I. Organizational Model/Violent Arrests

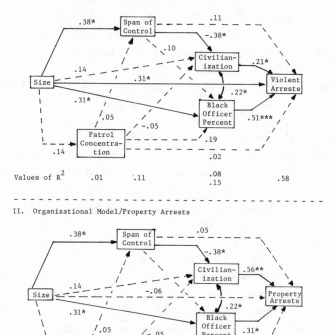

Figure 2.4. Pure Organizational and Environmental Models of Arrest Rates

urbanization and the character of the decisionmaking structure in the larger community are important determinants of police legalism, it would be inappropriate to make too much as yet of these substantive results. The problem of misspecification in the pure organizational model is more than a theoretical possibility. Consider that among the 42 cities studied here more urbanized communities have larger police agencies ($r = .76$) and agencies with higher proportions of black officers ($r = .73$). Neither finding is surprising, but both suggest that the impact of relative presence of minority police officers on police legalism may be at least somewhat artifactual. While no other correlations between the environmental and organizational variables exam-

III. Environmental Model/Violent Arrests

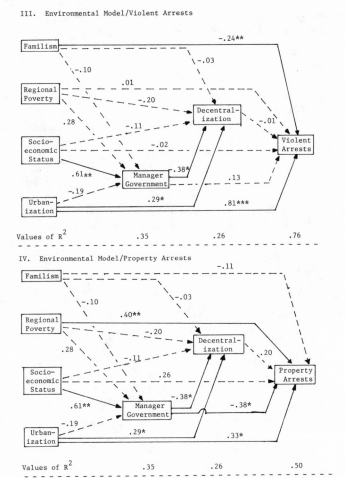

Values of R^2 .35   .26   .76

IV. Environmental Model/Property Arrests

Values of R^2 .35   .26   .50

* Significant at p < .05   ** Significant at p < .01.

Figure 2.4. (*Continued*)

ined here are as strong as these, others do exist to reinforce the suggestion.

The findings displayed in table 2.2 speak to this issue and resolve the ambiguities. They represent the results of two multiple regression procedures, one for each type of arrest rate. In each of these procedures, all organizational and environmental variables are included simultaneously as predictors. Because these regression analyses use

Table 2.2. Regression Results for Arrest Rates with All Independent Variables Entered

Independent Variables:	B	Std. Error of B	R² Change
I. Violent Crimes			
Familism	−1.920	1.326	.040
Regional Poverty	−.371	1.445	.000
Socioeconomic Status	−.138	1.677	.000
Urbanization	17.851**	2.725	.767
Manager Government	.930	3.229	.000
Political Decentralization	.027	.104	.000
Police Agency Size	−.008*	.003	.014
Patrol Concentration	.155	.155	.004
Span of Control	9.866*	3.950	.026
Civilianization	.400*	.156	.021
Black Police Presence	−.156	.269	.002

R^2 for Full Equation $=$ .874

	B	Std. Error of B	R² Change
II. Property Crimes			
Familism	2.795	4.664	.003
Regional Poverty	11.270*	5.085	.033
Socioeconomic Status	8.363	5.902	.011
Urbanization	30.645**	9.587	.113
Manager Government	22.034*	11.340	.086
Political Decentralization	.838*	.365	.037
Police Agency Size	−.028*	.011	.043
Patrol Concentration	.571	.544	.009
Span of Control	21.342	13.898	.013
Civilianization	1.917**	.548	.365
Black Police Presence	−1.203	.947	.010

R^2 for Full Equation $=$ .723

* Significant at $p < .05$.
** Significant at $p < .01$.

up a sizable number of degrees of freedom, they make it more difficult for the individual variables to attain statistical significance, and thus constitute a conservative test of their differential importance in predicting types and degrees of arrest-indexed police legalism.

Given the values of R^2 that were displayed in figure 2.4, it comes as no surprise to find in table 2.2 that, once again, variance in the violent arrest rates is more thoroughly and completely explained in this summary regression than is that in property arrest rates. What is more notable in this regard is that both relevant values of R^2 in table 2.2 are markedly higher than were the counterpart values produced by any of the pure models. This suggests, of course, that both environmental and organizational dynamics contribute in significant ways to the production of the legalistic police style, as that is reflected in arrest rates.[1]

The results displayed in table 2.2 lend further credence to the idea that the two kinds of arrest rates of interest here are indicators of different degrees, rather than of radically different types, of police legalism. Support for this contention comes from the fact that the findings from the two regression analyses share a certain core commonality upon which are then superimposed peculiarities specific to the types of arrests of interest. In both models, more urbanized communities are policed more legalistically, a finding confirming Black's (1976, 1980) proposition that formal social control must substitute for informal in large, diverse, and anonymous settings like major cities. Likewise, in both models, more civilianized police departments also police more legalistically, suggesting that the agencies that employ them use civilians for low-priority organizational maintenance tasks, freeing sworn officers for street-level patrol work and "crime-fighting." Finally, in both models it appears that, once other factors are controlled, larger police departments are less legalistic than their smaller counterparts. This is not, of course, what the pure organizational models of policing led us to believe, but those models did not account for the empirical link between big cities and big police departments. Controlling for that link, as is done here, suggests that larger departments are freer to define for themselves and to pursue missions other than or in addition to pure law enforcement.

There is only one substantive point to add to these general findings when the focus of attention centers on arrests for violent crimes and, interestingly enough, that addition comes from an organizational factor. When police are less intensively supervised—when the average number of officers per sergeant is relatively large—higher rates of arrests for violent crimes are registered. This finding makes good intuitive sense. If the natural propensity of police is to think of themselves and to advertise themselves to the general public as crimefighters, one would quite reasonably expect them to use whatever street-level discretion they enjoy while on duty to play that role by conducting investigations and making arrests. Such discretion, in turn, must be wider the less intensively officers are supervised by their sergeants, and that supervision must indeed be less intensive when those sergeants are responsible for larger numbers of officers.

When we focus on arrest rates for property crimes, a striking set of findings emerges from the analysis. First of all, the organizational measures used here contribute significantly more as a group to the explanatory model (total R^2 contribution $= .439$) than do their environmental counterparts (total R^2 contribution $= .283$). In light of the argument made earlier that the arrest rate for property crimes may well be a better measure of the police legalistic style, the importance of organizational dynamics for generating that style seems self-evident from these results. Beyond that, however, it is worth noting that nearly half of the environmentally explained variance in this model (R^2 contribution $= .123$) comes from the two measures of local political structure; the legalistic police style is more pronounced in cities governed by appointed city managers, and in those cities where political decisionmaking is more decentralized.

Two somewhat different, albeit related, dynamics are probably at work here. If we equate the legalistic style with police "professionalism"—an arguable equation on sociological grounds, but one made readily by police officers and executives—then these findings are consistent with an argument suggesting that the claim to professional status and the structuring of professional work are used as a buffer between police agencies and other actors in their urban environments. On the one hand, appointed managers demand and get legalistic policing as a part of the nonpolitical, scientific ethos that has been used to legitimize the council-manager plan since its very inception (Hofstadter 1955; Hays 1964). By doing so, they distance their police agencies from direct environmental influences and demands. On the other hand, police also adopt the legalistic, professional stance to buffer themselves from environments where power and influence are widely distributed across a plethora of urban actors and where responsiveness to one can be readily challenged by the others as preferential treatment. Officers may well carry personal preferences for the legalistic police style, and may well exercise those whenever supervisory realities in their departments allow them to do so; these findings suggest that that style has additional, latent functions in turbulent urban environments that make it a preferred choice among police agencies as well.

Conclusions and Caveats

Are police organizational dynamics important in their own right in the production of legalistic policing in American cities? The answer generated by this analysis would appear to be an affirmative one. The relative magnitude of their contribution varies from one measure of police legalism to another, but in no case is it negligible; by some lights, organization is even more critical than environment in generating the legalistic police style, with its focus on law enforcement and criminal apprehension. Within the constraints that do and must attach to a city-level analysis of police styles, the "burden of proof" noted earlier as falling on the shoulders of those who would argue for the importance of organizational factors in the determination of police style seems quite adequately met by the results of this exercise.

While that may be so, the issue cannot be said to be definitively resolved. This analysis is and can only be an introductory one, for the constraints that it faces are significant. Those constraints stem primarily from matters of measurement and research design—probably unavoidable in a city-level analysis but problematic nonetheless. An extended word about them is in order.

The measurement issue is one we have already noted, but it bears repeating: an arrest rate is at best only a component of the legalistic police style. It is surely not an equivalent. Findings from an analysis of arrest rates used as indicators of legalism are suggestive, not confirmatory. A thorough probing of the factors that produce the legalistic style requires data that better capture the variety of tasks associated with it and, for that matter, with the other varieties of style as well.

The second constraint on the findings reported above stems from an issue of research design, specifically from the issue of whether cities are the most appropriate units of analysis. It is arguable that they are not. Wilson (1972) posited police style as an organizational characteristic, an assumption with which a city-level analysis is surely consistent. But that is the problem: Wilson's assumption is merely that—and an uneasy one to boot. Despite the wide discretion most police officers enjoy in carrying out their duties, few people would argue that they are completely free agents; their actions are clearly patterned and some would even say determined by other social phenomena. The problem is to locate those other phenomena, and a plausible place to look is at the beat or neighborhood level. Practices vary from agency to agency, but most police officers patrol relatively circumscribed beats on a fairly regular basis. Similarly, most detectives find themselves returning to familiar areas to conduct their investigations. These beats and areas, in turn, vary in social, demographic, and economic composition; Duncan Timms' (1971) description of the city as an "urban mosaic" expresses this fact quite well. An ecologically informed argument for the situational or environmental determination of policing would see these beat-level or neighborhood-level characteristics as critical causal factors. For all practical purposes, a city-level analysis necessarily masks them; its findings may well fall subject to the well-known problem of "ecological correlation" (Robinson 1950).

Both of these measurement and design issues need resolving. The empirical findings presented in this chapter can stand as circumstantial evidence toward an argument for the importance of organizational factors in generating the legalistic police style; even more, they offer a set of data-based hypotheses deserving detailed tests in a study that can resolve those issues. All told, then, the analyses reported to this point are only a necessary and not a sufficient step toward a resolution of the organization-versus-environment issue in the study of police style. It is toward such a sufficient step that the remainder of this book is directed.

Note

1. This is further verified by a series of tests of the significance of increments to R^2 uniquely contributed by each of the environmental and organizational blocks of variables to each of the arrest rate predictive equations. For each block in each equation, the contributions were in fact significant at $p < .05$.

3. Police Styles in Urban Neighborhoods: Research Settings and Guiding Hypotheses

City-level studies of police style are appealing, almost alluring, for an empirical researcher. As a general rule, the wealth of data that are readily and continuously available on cities makes it possible to build sizable samples, use powerful techniques of statistical analysis, and uncover results that are reliably generalizable to urban areas beyond those immediately studied. All of this presumes, of course, that the available data speak to the issue at hand and that the city is indeed the appropriate setting for the conduct of such studies. As we have seen, however, neither presumption seems particularly warranted when the issue to be resolved is that of the differential effects of organization and environment in generating police working styles.

To take seriously the objections to city-level studies of police style as detailed in the previous chapter is, in effect, to demand and define a different research approach to the problem at hand. Such an approach would ideally still seek to work with a multiple of cities, preferably a strictly drawn random sample, and with measures of the structural character of each of their respective police departments. The approach would ideally differ from that of a typical city-level study, however, in that each city included in the sample it studied would be differentiable into a set of component police beats or neighborhoods, for each of which situational or environmental data would then be gathered. Similarly, data on police styles—with, obviously, an appropriate resolution of the attendant issues of their definition and operationalization—would be gathered for each of those same neighborhood units. The logic of inquiry would then be relatively straightforward. Police styles could reliably be tied to organizational dynamics if each of two conditions were met: (1) within-city variations on the critical dimensions of the styles were minimal while across-city variations were maximal, and (2) differences across cities on those same critical dimensions of style corresponded to differences in the natures of their police organizations and not generally to differences in their environmental characteristics. The argument for the situational determination of policing would be upheld if the converse of each condition were to emerge from the analysis.

The study which forms the basis for most of the remainder of this book was designed to be consistent with this logic of inquiry. It is necessarily more limited than the ideal research project depicted above, primarily because it focuses only on three specific cities: Elyria, Ohio, Columbia, South Carolina, and Newark, New Jersey. Collectively, these three offer a total of 50 geographical patrol beats for which data on neighborhood character and police style were collected and analyzed. Information on the structure of the police department in each city was also gathered for this research, as was information on the character of the city as a whole, and personal observations of working patrol officers and detectives in each were made as well. In a nutshell, then, this study was designed pragmatically to constitute a smaller version of what the larger and more desirable ideal would look like.

The data on police styles in each of these three cities and in each of their constituent police beats come not from the actual, on-site observations of police work conducted in each but rather from the records of police action compiled in the dispatch logs maintained in each police department.[1] This is something of a new departure, for most studies of police work conducted below the city level of analysis rely for their data on either direct observations of selected police officers' activities or responses of sampled officers to surveys or questionnaires. We will discuss in great detail in the following chapter the strengths and limitations of dispatch logs as sources of valid, reliable data for research; for now, suffice it to say that this procedure makes available a large quantity of data on police work. In all three cities, we will be working with better than 23,000 incidents of police action. Since city officials and police officers in all three cities make use of explicit territorial subdivisions in their work, and since the police incidents recorded in the dispatch logs are traceable to those territories, the need for data that can be aggregated to neighborhood levels of analysis is satisfied by these materials. Further, the U.S. Census provides ample measures of the social, demographic, and economic character of the territories in question. As a result, we can come quite close to our ideal study here with regard to collecting and working with measures of neighborhood-level police and nonpolice phenomena that are reasonably comparable across a selection of cities and their constituent internal units.

Elyria, Columbia, and Newark were selected for detailed analysis here on the basis of what I will call "designed happenstance". The availability to me in each city of extensive and reasonably comparable bodies of data on police work constitutes the happenstance. Although they offer a range of study sites that very quite nicely in, for example, size and geographical location, these three cities do not constitute a sample of some larger universe in any meaningful technical sense. They are, however, cities of the size and type that are included in the National Opinion Research Center's Permanent Community Sample; in fact, Newark was included among the 42 cities analyzed in the prior chapter. Herein lies the "design" noted above; police data available to me from other communities that could not have fallen into the Permanent Community Sample were not included as part of this research. That still does not make Elyria, Columbia, and Newark a sample in any scientific sense, but it does mean that any suggestions or hypotheses about police style offered by the findings from the analysis in the prior chapter can be directly extended to and tested in these specific sites.

Case studies are notoriously difficult to evaluate for the validity, reliability, and generality of their findings if one has no feel for how the sites of those studies compare to other places that might have been chosen as research settings. Accordingly, it is important to consider in some detail the character of each of the three cities of interest here as an urban setting and the basic structure of the municipal police department serving each. The remainder of this chapter is devoted to that task. We begin by treating each city separately, noting briefly its urban history and current character as well as the basic features of the police organization that serves it. That is followed by a comparative introduction to the form of local policing by assessing how urban community character determines police agency strength in each of the states containing one of our study sites, and how the sites themselves measure up to their respective statewide patterns. We conclude the chapter by culling from the analysis that it presents some hypotheses about the determination of police styles that can be added to those suggested by the city-level study reported in chapter 2 and that will be further tested in subsequent chapters.

Study Site No. 1: Elyria, Ohio

A community of approximately 60,000 people, Elyria is an old city in northeastern Ohio, situated about 25 miles west-southwest of Cleveland. It is a city with a long history. Founded in 1817 by Herman Ely, Elyria was incorporated as a municipality in 1833. During its early years, the community served as a stop on the underground railroad for runaway slaves. Elyria became an industrial city at approximately the time of the Civil War and largely remains one today. A major foundry is located within its borders, on the outskirts of the downtown business district. Auto, rubber, and steel plants in outlying portions of the city and throughout Lorain County, in which Elyria lies, are additional centers of employment for local residents.

To call Elyria an industrial town is not to imply that its citizens are all industrial workers. To the contrary, Elyria has a diverse population. Extremes of wealth and poverty, of lifestyle preferences and practices characterize its citizenry. City officials have been heard to boast that one of Elyria's residential neighborhoods contains one of the highest concentrations of upper-income families in the state of Ohio; they are a bit more reticent about two other neighborhoods, where the other extreme prevails.

Despite its relative smallness, Elyria is in many ways typical of an old industrial city in America's Snowbelt—as its central business district well reflects. Elyria's downtown is the center of local finance and serves as the seat of both city and county government. With the opening of a number of new bars and clubs in the past few years, it is becoming a hub of local recreation as well. As a retail center, however, it has come on hard times. The recent opening of a major regional shopping center in the northwestern outskirts of town has cut markedly into the volume of downtown retail trade, and the prognosis for the future calls for continued contraction in this sector of the local economy. The recession of the early 1980s likewise has had a severe effect, further hammering the already troubled heavy industries in and around Elyria and thus reinforcing the prognosis for local economic contraction.

What residential growth and expansion there is in Elyria is generally occurring on the outskirts of the city, to the northeast and the southwest, and in both the residents are largely middle- or upper-class in socioeconomic status. The city contains two notable poverty pockets as well. One of those, located directly south of the downtown, is a low-rise, low-income housing project with a population almost entirely black. Neighborhood leaders claim their community is ignored by city officials and some police officers, in informal personal interviews, mentioned a reluctance to patrol the area unless specific calls for service are received. The other poverty pocket, immediately west-southwest of the central business district, is interracial; its population is about half black and half white, from Appalachia. During the 1970s, this area was the scene of a riot, precipitated by a police shooting of a black teenager. Antipathy between residents and police still runs high over the memory of those times.

These relatively unique features notwithstanding, the predominant characteristic of Elyria is its "averageness" as an Ohio town. This contention is buttressed by the data presented in table 3.1, where selected social and economic characteristics of Elyria are compared with the averages on those same measures for all Ohio cities with 1980 populations greater than 10,000. Comparisons are offered on both an absolute and a relative[2] basis. From them, it seems clear that Elyria has proportionally more young children among its population than the average Ohio community. It has a greater unemployment problem as well, unsurprising in a city where the basic economy is so heavily dependent on old, heavy industry. Otherwise, there is little to distinguish Elyria; it is a middle-income, "familistic" city of married couples and their children, with a relatively small local black minority. The magnitude of the local crime problem, as indicated by the rates of reported crime displayed in table 3.1, is particularly average.

The police department that must respond to this crime problem— of concern to local officials, regardless of its magnitude in comparison with other Ohio cities—and generally service the needs of the people of Elyria, is an organization of 76 persons, 68 of whom (89.5%) are sworn police officers. While the patrol officers in Elyria are assigned to duty in different sectors or beats, the department is nevertheless a

Table 3.1. Elyria and Ohio's Cities—Absolute and Relative Comparisons, 1980

Urban Characteristic	Statewide Average (N = 145)	Elyria (Absolute)	Elyria (Relative)
City Size	39,862	57,538	0.22
Percent of the Population That:			
has completed secondary schooling	70.2	67.3	−0.28
is unemployed	7.4	10.8	1.18
is black	6.8	13.0	0.51
are children aged 5 or younger	6.8	8.9	1.40
are adults aged 65 or older	11.5	9.2	−0.59
are married	59.9	61.2	0.19
Median Family Income	$21,861	$20,831	−0.23
Reported Crime Rates (Per 1000 Residents)			
Violent	4.0	4.3	0.09
Property	52.2	50.7	−0.07

territorially centralized organization. All police operations are conducted from one central headquarters building, located in downtown Elyria.

Elyria's Police Department is structurally a relatively simple organization. Overall responsibility for police affairs is vested in Elyria's popularly elected mayor, who serves a four-year term. Responsible to the mayor for departmental administration is the chief of police. Under the chief and his deputy, the organization is divided into three major divisions: patrol, investigation, and technical services. Of the complement of sworn officers, and excluding the two departmental executives, 54 are assigned to the patrol division, 12 work in investigation and 8 operate the technical services division. Based on this distribution, the index of dispersion—a measure commonly used in organizational analysis to indicate the degree of internal division of labor (see Rushing 1967; Pondy 1969)—takes on a value of .65.[3] As an organization, the Elyria Police Department has a moderate level of internal division of labor.

Nearly all American police departments are paramilitary organizations structured around a hierarchy of ranks. Elyria is no different in this regard. Excluding its police chief, the Elyria Police Department comprises three captains, eight lieutenants, seven sergeants, and 49 police officers. On the basis of these numbers, the department might be said to be shaped a bit more like an hourglass than a pyramid. Further, its supervisory ratios are highly uneven; where there are theoretically an average of seven officers reporting to every sergeant, there is slightly fewer than one sergeant reporting to each lieutenant and roughly three lieutenants per captain. In terms of its formal rank structure and the distribution of people in it, the agency is somewhat topheavy.

Elyria, then, presents us with the closest we will encounter in this study to policing in a "typical" small city. The town faces a notable industrial unemployment problem and its downtown retail business sector is projected to face contraction, but Elyria is otherwise very nearly average in Ohio in terms of its social and economic character and its reported local crime problem. It is served by a police department that is relatively small and territorially centralized, and that is structured around a somewhat topheavy rank hierarchy managing a division of labor relatively moderate in magnitude.

Study Site No. 2: Columbia, South Carolina

For its size, which in 1980 stood at slightly over 100,000 people, Columbia, South Carolina is functionally diverse in the extreme. It is the largest city in its state and for that reason alone is a symbolic focal point for many citizens throughout South Carolina. It is also a center of government, by virtue of its being a chartered municipality, a county seat, and the state capital. Columbia is an educational node as well, serving as the home of the University of South Carolina and seven other institutions of higher education. Further, Columbia is a military center of some importance. The presence nearby of the Fort Jackson Military Reservation has an important effect on the life of the city and its larger metropolitan area, one indicator of which is the status of the latter as reportedly the twentieth largest military market in the country.[4] In most respects, Columbia stands at the functional center of life in South Carolina.

Columbia's centrality in South Carolina's urban system is not a new development. Charleston, of course, was the premier city of colonial South Carolina but a hot and humid climate, swampy conditions, and regular assaults from disease propelled many South Carolinians to seek refuge from nature's ravages in upland and inland areas for sizable proportions of every year (Bridenbaugh, 1938, 1955). Columbia soon came to benefit from this patterned annual migration. Established as the capital of South Carolina in 1786, Columbia was chartered as an independent town in 1804 and from about that time began a slow but steady movement toward urban prominence in the state.

The Civil War, of course, interrupted Columbia's development in a radical way. General William Tecumseh Sherman's march to the sea turned northward after passing across Georgia and, in 1865, came to Columbia. Perhaps because of its status as capital of the state that had initially opened the armed hostilities, Columbia suffered proportionally as much war damage as did Atlanta, and more than most other Southern cities. It was virtually leveled by Sherman and his army. Rebuilding began shortly after their departure, but it was not until the latter part of the 1870s that Columbia could even be said to have returned to the *status quo ante*.

Since then, the story of Columbia has been one of relatively uninterrupted growth and progress, initially as a governmental center and transportation hub and more recently as a cultural, military and industrial node. Columbia has benefited markedly from the general rise of the Sunbelt; between 1960 and 1970 alone, the city's population grew by roughly 16.5 percent while that of its metropolitan area expanded at better than double that rate. City growth tapered off during the subsequent decade but metropolitan growth did not. Thus, Columbia stands at the center of an increasingly large and diverse urban system.

Where Elyria is relatively typical of other communities in Ohio with regard to its urban character and its reported local crime rate, Columbia is exceedingly atypical of other urban communities in South Carolina. Table 3.2 uses the same format as table 3.1 to present data in support of that contention. A methodological note is in order here. The statewide averages for South Carolina displayed in table 3.2 are

Table 3.2. Columbia and South Carolina's Cities—
Absolute and Relative Comparisons, 1980

Urban Characteristics	Statewide Averages (N = 20)	Columbia (Absolute)	Columbia (Relative)
City Size	27,952	101,208	3.07
Percent of the Population That:			
has completed secondary schooling	53.9	63.8	1.10
is unemployed	6.6	6.7	0.07
is black	34.9	40.2	0.41
are children aged 5 or younger	6.8	5.3	-1.88
are adults aged 65 or older	12.0	10.4	-0.59
are married	56.3	40.5	-2.39
Median Family Income	$16,668	$15,964	-0.50
Reported Crime Rates (Per 1000 Residents)			
Violent	10.2	18.1	1.80
Property	71.6	126.4	2.26

computed on a base of 20 communities with populations at or above 10,000 persons as of 1980. Accordingly, those figures and the relative measures of Columbia's characteristics are not particularly stable; the relative comparisons should be characterized by greater fluctuations about the grand mean than was the case with the comparable figures used in the Ohio analysis. Even granting that, however, table 3.2 nonetheless demonstrates that Columbia is far from typical of urban South Carolina on almost every variable measured.

Simply as a matter of course, we would expect that a large city would be different in social, economic and demographic terms from the smaller ones around it, but Columbia's relative uniqueness would appear to be rooted more in its functional complexity than it its sheer size. Relative to other cities in South Carolina, Columbia has a markedly more educated population that is *not* disproportionately young or old or married but, in fact, the reverse with regard to all three. The causal factor here is undoubtedly the presence in the city of the large number of institutions that attract, employ, and service single, educated young adults: the state university and the other local colleges, the state legislature and the capital's official government bureaucracies, the county and city bureaucracies, and the military base. The city is relatively unique in terms of the general social and economic characteristics of its population in large part because it is big, but in much larger part because it is institutionally and functionally complex.

A long line of theory in urban sociology (Wirth 1938; Simmel 1903) suggests that a necessary byproduct of the process of urbanization is the breakdown of premodern moral codes for the regulation of social behavior, resulting in an attendant rise in the rates of social deviance of all types. The reported crime rates displayed in table 3.2 are consistent with this line of interpretation. The reported crime rates for Columbia may not themselves be radically disproportionate; after all, Columbia is three standard deviations above the statewide average in terms of city size, while its reported crime rates are something less than that. Nonetheless, to the extent that reported crime rates measure victimization risk,[5] the citizens of Columbia are in a good deal more jeopardy relative to other South Carolinians than are the citizens of Elyria relative to other Ohioans.

The Columbia Police Department is comparable to its counterpart agency in Elyria only in being territorially centralized in one downtown headquarters building. Even here, however, the similarity is relatively superficial, for the Columbia police pay a fair amount of attention to geography by defining 16 distinct patrol beats. Beyond that, however, the department is larger and more internally complex, and its rank hierarchy is somewhat different as well.

The Columbia Police Department is an organization of 276 persons, of whom 212 (76.8%) are sworn police officers. Two of those officers are departmental executives: the chief of police and his deputy. In Columbia, the police chief is directly responsible to a city manager who is appointed by and serves at the pleasure of the elected city council. Under the chief and his deputy, the remaining officers in the police department are distributed among five major organizational divisions: records, training and community relations, investigation, uniformed (or patrol), and services. By far the largest of those is the uniformed division, accounting for 81.6 percent of the sworn complement. Investigations is the second largest division with 14.6 percent of the sworn employees, while services, training and records account for the remaining 1.9, 1.4 and 0.4 percent of the force, respectively. Calculating the index of dispersion across all five of the divisions yields a value of .39; even across a truncated uniformed/investigation/other trichotomy, the calculated value of D rises only marginally to .47. Whichever figure we use, the Columbia Police Department is characterized by a less complex internal division of labor than was true of its counterpart in Elyria.

The police department in Columbia has a rank hierarchy that is somewhat atypical for American policing in general. It includes the rank of corporal positioned, as in the army, between sergeants and patrol officers (privates). The rank is little more than honorific; in Columbia, as in most other police agencies, the sergeants are the first-line supervisors of all below them in the rank hierarchy, while corporals exercise no supervisory authority over the patrol officers below them. In any event, the rank hierarchy under the chief and his deputy consists of by 5 captains, 10 lieutenants, 16 sergeants, 20 corporals and 159 patrol officers. This is a relatively steep pyramidal structure which imposes a larger responsibility on lower than on higher level supervisors. Note that at the ranks of sergeant and above, theoretically no more than two people report to any one higher-ranking supervisor. Sergeants, however, are responsible for an average of one corporal and approximately ten officers each.

Where Elyria was typical, then, Columbia is unique—a status attributable more to its extreme functional diversity than to its size. Being located in America's Sunbelt, it lies in a growing, thriving economic setting; being a functionally elaborate place, it attracts a sizable population of relatively well-educated, upwardly mobile, unmarried young people. With them comes a statistically notable crime problem which is made the special preserve of a moderately large police department with a complex rank hierarchy and organizational structure, but with a relatively low degree of internal division of labor. In contrast to Elyria, Columbia focuses proportionately more of its officers and its attention on street patrol and the local crime problem.

Study Site No. 3: Newark, New Jersey

In the spring of 1982, the people of Newark went to the polls to elect (as it turned out, to reelect) a mayor. One of those campaigning for the post had summarized life in Newark shortly before the election in the following words: "Ken Gibson [the incumbent mayor] once said that wherever American cities are going, Newark will get there first. Well, we've been there and we've found that it's a mighty hot place." Perhaps too extreme an assessment, his statement nonetheless captures a tragic truth about the current state of the city. Life in Newark is hard; both the city and its police department have lived through a very difficult time, and the prognosis for the future offers only a few glimmers of hope.

Newark's population is the largest of the three cities being studied here, with a 1980 U.S. Census count of approximately 329,000 people. It is also the oldest of the three cities. Settlement in the area actually dates back to the mid-seventeenth century; 1666 is the year attributed to the city's founding. From its early days as a port and commercial center, Newark rather quickly became transformed into a craftsman's and, ultimately, a manufacturer's city. It achieved no little success in this last capacity, mounting a highly regarded industrial exposition in 1872 which exhibited to the rest of the nation and to foreign visitors alike a wide range of high-quality, locally manufactured goods.

Without meaning to slight urban history generally or Newark's urban history in particular, it is nonetheless fair to focus this introduction most heavily on the period since approximately 1950—the time during which Newark has become emblematic of the plight of America's old cities in the Snowbelt. Population shrinkage, business relocation, and job loss have hit Newark particularly hard. The city had approximately 440,000 residents in 1950, but the count has declined consistently with every subsequent census. Jobs have moved out with concomitant speed; the Prudential Insurance Company, Newark's leading corporation and a prime mover in the city's efforts at downtown revitalization, cut its local home office staff from roughly 14,000 in 1945 to approximately 4000 in 1978. Urban deconcentration in America's northeast is, of course, nothing new (Berry, ed. 1976), but figures such as these tend to stand out above the general trend.

The most important event in Newark's history may well have been the urban disorder it experienced in 1967. As the figures noted above suggest, the 1967 riot did not cause residents—and employers—to flee Newark; they had been doing so for some time. Nonetheless, there is evidence that the disorders of 1967, one of the most severe to rack an American city in that year (Downes 1968) accelerated both; that it promoted a massive white flight from the city; that it generated notably higher crime rates in subsequent years (Slovak 1983); that it contributed directly to the election of Newark's first black mayor, Kenneth Gibson, in 1970 and thus indirectly to the appointment of its first black police director, Hubert Williams, in 1974; that, in short, it changed the social and political structure of the city in radical ways while it accelerated equally radical demographic changes.

Today, Newark is a city in trouble. Like Columbia, it is the largest city in its state and, while not the capital of New Jersey is nonetheless an important governmental and educational center. Unlike Columbia, Newark has not attracted to itself an educated, upwardly mobile population of young adults. Quite the contrary is the case, as table 3.3 demonstrates. Relative to the 118 New Jersey communities with populations of 10,000 or more persons in 1980, Newark's population falls far below statewide averages with regard to its educational and income levels and its proportion of married adults, and far above them with regard to local proportions of blacks, young children, and the unemployed. Of course, Newark is not one vast sea of urban desolation. In parts of its north side Forest Hills area, Italian culture is alive and well and reminiscent in its cohesiveness of patterns described by Gans in Boston (1962) and Suttles in Chicago (1968). In the southeastern Ironbound section, a predominantly Portuguese population has adopted a self-reliant "bootstraps" strategy for neighborhood revitalization and has achieved marked economic success and social cohesion as a result. In other parts of the city, middle-class black residents struggle for personal security and neighborhood stability. Nonetheless, where Columbia emerged from our analysis as a reasonably thriving city, Newark emerges as an obviously troubled one.

Table 3.3 suggests that violent crime is particularly problematic in Newark. While the impression is accurate enough, it is nothing new. Newark's reported homicide rate has consistently exceeded that of most other large American cities since the early 1970s, and the levels of fear registered by its residents in victimization surveys have been consistently high relative to those recorded in other major cities in comparable research efforts (U.S. Department of Justice 1976). Public life in Newark is and is perceived to be a threatening affair.

Table 3.3. Newark and New Jersey's Cities—Absolute and Relative Comparisons, 1980

Urban Characteristic	Statewide Averages (N = 118)	Newark (Absolute)	Newark (Relative)
City Size	29,060	329,248	7.61
Percent of the Population That:			
has completed secondary schooling	66.5	44.6	− 1.75
is unemployed	6.5	13.4	2.65
is black	10.8	58.2	2.86
are children aged 5 or younger	5.7	8.6	2.07
are adults aged 65 or older	12.7	8.8	− 0.98
are married	57.7	48.3	− 1.40
Median Family Income	$23,229	$11,989	− 1.92
Reported Crime Rates (Per 1000 Residents)			
Violent	5.0	34.1	4.41
Property	58.8	94.9	1.06

At the top executive level, administration of the Newark Police Department includes an organizational layer not encountered in either Columbia or Elyria or, for that matter, in the majority of American cities. The elected mayor of Newark, in whom ultimate responsibility for the department lies, delegates executive authority to an appointed police director, who serves as the department's chief administrator at the pleasure of the mayor. Some staff functions—most notably planning, internal affairs, and media relations—center around and report directly to the police director. Direct administrative responsibility for daily police operations, however, is delegated from the director downward to the chief of police, under whom fall the various divisions and bureaus of the department. This is the most elaborate administrative apparatus for policing we have encountered for this research.

Table 3.4. Personnel Changes in the Newark Police
Department, 1970–1980

Year	Total Personnel	Total Sworn Officers	Percent Sworn Officers
1970	1702	1445	84.9
1971	1722	1461	84.8
1972	1477	1256	85.0
1973	1830	1501	82.0
1974	1786	1603	89.8
1975	1854	1588	85.7
1976	1640	1502	91.6
1977	1741	1457	83.7
1978	1722	1447	84.0
1979	1454	1192	82.0
1980	1189	930	78.2

It is a good deal more difficult to offer a simple summary of policing in Newark than it is in either Elyria or Columbia, where the police departments have remained fairly stable over the past few years, police complements have changed little and even those changes have been incremental and predictable. In Newark, quite the contrary is the case. Between 1970 and 1980, the total size of the department fluctuated widely, as the figures displayed in table 3.4 demonstrate. In the early years of the decade, the department grew with the influx of funds from Washington and Trenton for special anti-crime experimental programs; in the later years, those sources of funds dried up and could not be replaced locally, as the city government was generally undergoing its own financial crisis. As a result, Newark earned yet another dubious distinction; it became one of the first cities in America to achieve retrenchment in policing by means of sizable direct layoffs, which befell the department in 1975 and 1976, and especially—with the layoff of 200 officers—in 1978. The replacement pool created by these layoffs was such that the Newark Police Department did not accept or train new recruits in its police academy between 1975 and 1981; it simply did not need them, given the number of laid off police awaiting their return to active duty, to fill vacancies in its reduced complement.

While the size of the Newark Police Department changed during the 1970s, so also did its structure as a formal organization. In 1975, the agency was organized into five major divisions: detective, patrol, investigations, traffic, and staff services. In 1981, the number of divisions remained at five, but: the old detective and investigation divisions were merged into one; the old traffic division was reduced in size and scope to the status of a bureau of the patrol division; staff services remained as a division, but many of its functions were split off into a new records and communications division; and a new youth and community services division was created, virtually from "scratch." Further, the structure of the organization became a good deal more elaborate during the same time period. The 62 separate bureaus, desks, or sections of which the five general divisions had been composed in 1975 had increased to 74 by 1981.

As a result of all of these changes, it is difficult to present data on division of labor in the Newark Police Department or the dimensions of its rank hierarchy and feel confident that those are not overly skewed by a layoff or a recent organizational shakeup. The picture as of 1976 is probably as good as any. It predates the organizational restructuring noted above and two of the three layoffs as well, especially the massive one of December 1978. In any event, as of 1976, 62.0 percent of the sworn complement were allocated to the patrol division, 12.8 percent to detectives, and 12.6 percent to staff services, with traffic and investigations making up the remainder (with 8.5% and 4.1% of the total of sworn officers, respectively). Calculating the index of dispersion on this divisional basis yields a result of $D = .72$. This is the highest index value attained in any of our three study sites; of the three police departments of interest here, that in Newark houses the most complex internal allocation of personnel across major organizational units.

In that same base year of 1976, Newark's police rank hierarchy was relatively pyramidal, housing (below the executive level) 28 captains, 108 lieutenants, 116 sergeants, 212 detectives and 1011 police officers. As in Columbia, these figures yield in Newark a relatively low supervisory ratio above the rank of sergeant—with the highest figure in this regard being a theoretical average of four lieutenants reporting to each captain—but a relatively high ratio for sergeants themselves, with figures of 8.7 or 10.5 officers theoretically reporting to each, depending on whether detectives are or are not included in the count. In regard to street-level supervisory span of control, Newark stands a good deal closer to Columbia than to Elyria.

Clearly, layoffs and structural changes notwithstanding, the Newark Police Department takes territorial decentralization quite seriously. The department is administered from a central headquarters building in downtown Newark, which houses many of the organization's service functions. The patrol force is distributed among four district stations, each of which in turn divides the area for which it is responsible into seven patrol sectors or beats. The patrol division headquarters staff and the tactical squads share a separate building from those district stations and from the downtown headquarters building, while the training academy is located in still another building and the central repair garage in yet another. Such territorial decentralization is unlike anything encountered in our other study sites. It is, in a sense, a function of the state of the city, where structural abandonment is not simply a phenomenon but rather a plague. In such a setting, space is hardly at a premium, a fact of which the Newark Police Department clearly has taken advantage.

Like Columbia but unlike Elyria, Newark is typical of very little compared with other communities in its state. Unlike Columbia, however, its atypicality does not work to its advantage. Poverty, physical dilapidation, and violence characterize this declining industrial city, so that its city government and police department are faced with one crisis after another. That police department—relatively large, structurally complex, territorially decentralized, and constantly shrinking—faces the most vexing urban environment of any studied in detail here and, perhaps, of any to be encountered in a large American city in the contemporary era.

The Determinants of Local Police Strength:
A Comparative Assessment

As introductions to comparative case study research, narratives definitely have their limits. Even when they follow a standard format and focus on a limited set of variables measured in each place described, narratives tend nonetheless to emphasize and perhaps to magnify the particular or the idiosyncratic and to mask what might otherwise be quite ordinary about the places they describe. The narrative descriptions of Elyria, Columbia and Newark offered here are no exception in this regard. The functional complexity of the city of Columbia and the turmoil recently experienced in the Newark Police Department are, after all, relatively notable; narrative descriptions of both places would be seriously remiss in declining to mention them. Having focused sufficiently on such factors, however, it is time to put each of these cities into their respective contexts as elements of larger urban systems in which similar problems of policing are faced by all elements and in which common norms or rules of policing may apply.

To do that, we turn to a more general assessment of the norms by which police strength is determined in cities in each of the states where our case study cities are situated. While urban systems need not be coterminous with state boundaries, it is nonetheless true that, for example, police powers, minimum standards for police training, criminal statutes to be enforced by police, and civil service provisions governing the terms of employment of police officers are determined by state legislatures. The use of state boundaries to define urban systems is therefore by no means unreasonable.

Police strength is a relatively formal dimension of policing on which to fix. There is no necessary correlation between either absolute or relative police strength and general police style—at least none that suggests itself from the scholarly literature. There is nonetheless good reason to focus on the determinants of police department size as an introduction to our subsequent analyses of police style. Consider only the following.

In research on nonpolice organizations, absolute size has long been recognized (Rushing 1967; Pondy 1969; and for a more general treatment, Hage 1980) as a causal trigger for increasing organizational complexity, administrative intensity, division of labor and diversity of work product. In the police realm, Michael Brown (1981) has argued, with some empirical backing from his own research, that there is a causal relationship between size and officer discretion: the larger the police department, the freer the officer to exercise discretion in encounters with citizens. If the natural propensity of police officers is toward a more legalistic police style, as was suggested by some of the findings presented in the prior chapter, then an analysis of the determinants of police department size in these three study sites and others in their respective states may offer suggestive evidence on the determination of the legalistic police working style.

In addition, critics of American policing have long chastised city and police officials for "throwing people at problems," charging that cities attempt to meet their crime problems by simply and mechanistically hiring more police. (See Heinz, Jacob and Lineberry 1983 or Caiden 1977.) We can to some degree assess the validity of the charge by examining on an empirical basis the causal effects which produce larger urban police agencies in each of the states where our study sites are located.

Finally, relative police strength (defined as the number of police per population increment in a given community) has made recent appearances in the sociological literature (Jacobs 1979; Liska, Lawrence, and Benson 1981) as an indicator of police visibility and, as such, has been tied to various social and economic characteristics of American cities as a mechanism by means of which the resourceful enjoy the capacity to control the resourceless. This emphasis on direct control is arguably related to the police style that Wilson (1972) labeled legalistic, although it is worth noting in this regard that Liska and Chamlin (1984) found no empirical link in the sample of cities they studied between relative police strength and arrest rates after the introduction of appropriate control variables. Given the uncertainty that surrounds the appropriate measurement procedures to be applied to the concept of police style, it seems worthwhile to conduct a limited replication of the Jacobs effort here as an alternative city-level introduction to the legalistic police style and its production—one tied directly to the cities on which the remainder of this study will focus.

For all of these reasons, an assessment of the determinants of local police strength seems a fitting manner in which to bring to a close this introduction to policing and to urban life in Elyria, Columbia, and Newark.[6]

In what follows, we will use the same social and economic indicators of community status discussed above to assess the determinants of municipal police department size in communities in Ohio, South Carolina, and New Jersey as of 1980. In so doing, we hope to uncover the "normative formulae" used by city and police officials in each state as they make their decisions to allocate resources to the task of local policing, and to compare the substances of those formulae across states. Along the way, we will also assess the degree to which each of our specific study sites is over- or under-policed, relative to the general situation in its respective state.

Absolute Strength. As noted above, critics of American policing have charged that the official response to urban crime has been little more than a mechanistic hiring of additional police officers. Were the criticisms valid, we would anticipate an empirical link—specifically, a strong positive correlation—between police strength and reported crime rates. This expectation would hold despite the well-known limitations of reported crime rates as measures of actual crime levels, for it is the former that become public knowledge and serve as a justification for both public and police perceptions of local realities (Fishman 1978; Baker et al. 1983; Slovak 1983). There is indeed evidence for such a pattern in the correlation coefficients displayed in table 3.5, and that evidence emerges for all of the three states examined. Nonetheless, even stronger evidence emerges of a somewhat different lockstep approach to police organizational size. As of 1980, these correlational findings suggest that urban officials planned the sizes of their police departments as though there were an optimal agency size based almost totally on the size of the city to be served.

A methodological note is in order at this point. In all three of the states of interest here, the distributions of city size and of absolute police strength are characterized by a positive skew; in each state, one or a handful of cities takes on extremely high values on these measures, threatening to distort rather seriously any empirical results from an analysis using the skewed measures. A common statistical procedure for correcting for this problem is to take the logarithms of the skewed variables and use these transformed values in the analysis. The results of doing so in each state in this analysis are also depicted in table 3.5. As is clear from its coefficients, the transformations effect only minor changes in empirical results, and they leave untouched the substantive inferences to be made from those findings. Since it is highly unlikely that many people—police officials or otherwise—actually think about city or police department sizes in "adjusted" terms, and since the technical adjustments matter so little to the empirical results, this discussion will focus on the results of using untransformed measures of city and department size.

Many of the urban indicators discussed earlier are also correlated with police force size in cities in Ohio, New Jersey, and South Carolina. As might have been anticipated, wealthier cities and those most heavily populated by married couples tend to have smaller police departments; cities with larger black subpopulations and those suffering higher rates of unemployment tend to have larger ones. These tendencies are common in all three states, and are consistent with an

Table 3.5. The Correlates of Absolute Police Strength

	Absolute Police Strength In:					
	Ohio (N = 127)		South Carolina (N = 18)		New Jersey (N = 101)	
	Raw	Logged	Raw	Logged	Raw	Logged
City Size (Raw)	.966*	.837*	.965*	.909*	.969*	.783*
City Size (Logged)	.769*	.936*	.909*	.949*	.809*	.943*
Violent Crime Rate	.570*	.535*	.496*	.523*	.693*	.702*
Property Crime Rate	.312*	.361*	.706*	.741*	.411*	.546*
Median Family Income	−.226*	−.221*	−.134	−.172	−.465*	−.536*
Secondary Schooling	−.241*	−.248*	.490*	.531*	−.463*	−.534*
Unemployment	.218*	.298*	.003	.029	.555*	.598*
Black Population	.430*	.496*	.341	.391	.547*	.613*
Married Population	−.297*	−.309*	−.767*	−.731*	−.393*	−.498*
Child Population	.139	.194*	−.600*	−.474*	.439*	.451*
Elderly Population	.065	.122	−.218	−.173	−.050	.053

* = Significant at or below p = .05.

argument for the determination of police strength based on conflict theory. Nonetheless, in no instance do the magnitudes of the relevant coefficients exceed those for city size and at least one of the crime rates displayed in table 3.5. With regard to absolute police agency size, it seems that little more need be said about urban demography, ecology, or economy; city size and reported crime rates by and large tell the tale.

In communities in all three of the states studied here, city sizes and violent and property crime rates are positively correlated; the magnitudes of these relationships, while varying from state to state, range nonetheless from moderate to large. Further, the effects of partialling either crime rates or city sizes from the relationships with absolute police strength vary somewhat from state to state. As table 3.6 demonstrates, city sizes and police agency sizes remain heavily correlated despite controls for crime. When city size is the control, however, crime disappears from the picture altogether in South Carolina; both types of reported crime rates remain relevant in New Jersey; only violent crime appears to correlate with police strength in Ohio. These results suggest that something of a regional difference may distinguish local officials' police personnel planning. In the South, as exemplified by the South Carolina results, police department size seems solely and overwhelmingly a function of city size; in the industrial Northeast, as represented by Ohio and New Jersey, city officials look predominantly to city size in determining police personnel complements, but then increment their planned allocations further in accordance with reported crime rates.

Where do Elyria, Columbia, and Newark fit in all this? Compared with other cities in their respective states, are their police agencies the

Table 3.6. Partial Correlates of Absolute Police Strength

	Absolute Police Strengh In		
Correlate (Control)	Ohio	South Carolina	New Jersey
City Size (Violent Crime)	.949*	.952*	.952*
City Size (Property Crime)	.962*	.928*	.978*
Violent Crime (City Size)	.220*	.018	.437*
Property Crime (City Size)	.024	−.121	.646*

* = Significant at or below p = .05.

Table 3.7. Observed and Predicted Absolute Police
Strength

	Observed, 1980	Predicted, 1980	O - P Std. Error
Elyria, Ohio	76	98	-.36
Columbia, South Carolina	276	296	-.97
Newark, New Jersey	1189	1211	-.67

size that their city sizes and crime rates would lead one to anticipate?
To answer this question, multiple regression equations were constructed to predict police agency size in each of the three states, in
each case beginning with equations containing all ten predictors listed
in table 3.5 and then progressively deleting independent variables
until only those with statistically significant slopes remained. In South
Carolina, the only significant predictor of absolute police strength was
city size; in Ohio, city size and the reported violent crime rate remained in the final equation; in New Jersey, city size and the reported
property crime rate were the significant predictors. Inserting the actual sizes and crime rates for Elyria, Columbia, and Newark into their
appropriate state-level equations yields the predictions for police
strength displayed in table 3.7. With those also appear the actual
personnel complements in each police department as of 1980, with
the difference between the observed and the expected expressed in
terms of standard errors of the estimate. As the table demonstrates, all
three cases predict a police department larger than that actually observed, but uniformly within one standard error of the regression-
based prediction. Thus, all three of the cities on which we focus here
are "understaffed" in their police departments relative to other communities in their respective states, although none by all that much.

In terms of absolute local police strength, then, neither Elyria,
Columbia, nor Newark seem atypical of other urban communities in
their states. In none of the states is there evidence that urban officials
engineer police department sizes in a mechanistic response to crime
rates; in all three, however, it appears that the engineering is a mechanistic response to city size. Decisionmakers in each state have apparently determined what they see as an optimal size formula for police
agencies, which serves as a general norm for their police staffing
decisions. As research on police operations in America has uncovered

no empirical grounds for linking agency size with police effectiveness (Skogan 1976; Ostrom and Parks 1973), this rule has little to recommend it over the alternative of throwing people at problems. Its mathematical precision smacks more of a rough-and-ready scientism than of anything else.

In looking to a subsequent analysis of police styles within and among the neighborhoods of Elyria, Columbia, and Newark, these findings on the determinants of agency size offer something of a guiding hypothesis. As we have seen, there appears to be a regional difference at work in the determination of absolute police strength. Once they have responded to city size, the two northern agencies studied here (like others in their states) appear to add further personnel increments based on the magnitudes of their reported crime rates while the southern police department (like others in its state) apparently does not. This difference speaks in a general way to the distinction between the legalistic and the watchmanlike police styles. The former is more attuned to strict law enforcement among all community groups, and calls for officers who work within it to assume the role of crimefighter. The latter is, in turn, more attuned to a minimalistic definition of police work which calls for its officers to act as watchmen alert to possible breaches of informal community standards of order. A reasonable inference from this would be that departments that receive personnel increments in response to reported crime rates are, by virtue of that fact, intended to play more self-conscious and determined crime-suppression roles; those structured on the basis of city size alone are intended to respond to the simple likelihood that more people in a community mean more encounters among its citizens, which, in turn, mean more chances for conflicts and breaches of order, much along the lines suggested by classical sociologists of the city like Louis Wirth (1938). We have in the results of this analysis a reasonably strong suggestion that regional urban location and police style may well be associated. Absolute police strength in Elyria, Columbia, and Newark is quite satisfactorily predicted by the general decision rules operating in Ohio, South Carolina, and New Jersey. Accordingly, we might anticipate a relatively legalistic police style to characterize police work in the first and the third, and a more watchmanlike stance to typify that in the second.

Relative Strength. Relative police strength—that is, the number of police employees per thousand community residents—is a variable distinct both conceptually and empirically from its absolute counterpart. At the conceptual level, relative police strength implies less the simple size of the agency and more the visibility its members have among the populations they serve. The latter seems, in turn, a necessary condition delimiting the degree to which police can be intrusive in the run of social life, a key component of the legalistic policing style. At the empirical level, relative police strength is here only moderately correlated with either city or police department size, with respective coefficients in this regard of .059 and .259 in South Carolina (neither of which is statistically significant), .330 and .423 in Ohio, and .241 and .434 in New Jersey. Thus, this introduction can be rounded out by focusing separately on relative as well as absolute police strength.

In a study of relative police strength in 96 major metropolitan areas in both 1960 and 1970, David Jacobs (1979) discovered that income inequality was a major determinant of the dependent variable; the more unequal the metropolitan distribution of income, the higher the level of relative police strength. In his 1960 analysis, income inequality was rivaled only by the number of urban retail drug and liquor stores as a causal factor. By 1970, however, race and local crime rates also figured as positive determinants as, depending on the measurement conventions adopted, did unemployment and local population size. Jacobs interpreted his findings as evidence for a conflict theory of policing, wherein economic elites and selected small-business sectors pressure local officials for increasing amounts of visible police protection. That seems reasonable enough, given the measures he included in his analysis. It is worth noting, however, that for neither year studied did he include any measures designed to tap the familistic dimensions of metropolitan social structure and, through them, the conventional norms of family-maintenance and stability with which police are generally thought to be in agreement and by which they are often motivated in their routines and activities (Skolnick 1966; Niederhoffer 1969). In that the measures used in this analysis do include such items, it will be well worth noting whether and where these results diverge from Jacobs'.

Table 3.8. Correlates of Relative Police Strength

| | Relative Police Strength In | | | | | |
| | Ohio (N = 127) | | South Carolina (N = 18) | | New Jersey (N = 101) | |
	Raw	Logged	Raw	Logged	Raw	Logged
City Size (Raw)	.330*	.235*	.059	.105	.241*	.302*
City Size (Logged)	.182*	.132	.031	.080	.329*	.396*
Violent Crime Rate	.357*	.276*	.170	.236	.561*	.562*
Property Crime Rate	.340*	.269*	.098	.176	.793*	.700*
Median Family Income	−.110	−.088	.054	−.020	−.418*	−.432*
Secondary Schooling	−.199*	−.166*	.454*	.458*	−.349*	−.354*
Unemployment	.121	.119	.102	.142	.452*	.474*
Black Population	.335*	.262*	.267	.291	.483*	.513*
Married Population	−.090	−.028	−.008	−.066	−.495*	−.536*
Child Population	.068	.072	.129	.122	.187*	.248*
Elderly Population	.228*	.198*	.317	.293	.325*	.293*

* = Significant at or below p = .05.

Toward that end, table 3.8 displays the correlations between city size, crime rates and urban indicators and relative police strength in communities in Ohio, New Jersey, and South Carolina. Again, results based on both transformed and untransformed measures of city size and relative police visibility are displayed in the table. In this instance, the transformation produces somewhat different results from state to state. In general, Ohio coefficients are reduced somewhat by use of the logarithmic measures of police visibility and city size; in South Carolina and New Jersey, the effect—where there is one—is the opposite. The most practical course of action here is again to focus on the results using untransformed measures.

The coefficients displayed in table 3.8 suggest that the determinants of relative police strength are more numerous than and somewhat distinct from the set that served the same purpose for absolute police strength. City size, while positively correlated with police strength, is not the predominant element in the story; in each of the three states, other indicators generate coefficients that exceed those produced by size, and to a substantial degree. In South Carolina, educational attainment of the local population is notable in this regard; in Ohio, reported crime rates and community racial composition stand out; in New Jersey, virtually everything measured outperforms size in correlating with relative police strength.

Containing so few urban communities, South Carolina and its results are best excluded from any serious comparisons with Jacobs' earlier research, but Ohio and New Jersey are not so limited. Granting the ten-year lapse between collection times for Jacobs' measures and these, some commonalities do appear. The positive correlations between police visibility and city size, crime rates, and percent black as of 1980 are quite congruent with those offered by Jacobs (1979:919) for 1970. The importance of the age structure of the population is a finding unique to this effort, for Jacobs employed no such measure. Finally, where this research directly contradicts his is with regard to local socioeconomic status. His study yielded positive correlations between income and police strength; this analysis yields negative ones, especially in New Jersey. The difference may well be a result of the different units of analysis used in the two efforts. Where Jacobs studied major metropolitan areas, the communities analyzed here run the gamut in each of the subject states from small isolated towns through tranquil suburbs to major central cities, but include no metropolitan areas. America's metropolitan areas were heavily stratified by income in 1970 with central cities being notably poorer than their surrounding suburbs; that differential was generally even larger in 1980. As a result, the different correlations between police strength and income produced by these two efforts may not be contradictory, despite surface impressions. To exert social control most effectively over poor minority populations living predominantly in central cities, economic dominants—who are mostly suburban-dwellers—must lobby for larger central-city police forces. If successful in this, they will require relatively fewer police in their own residential communities. Kasarda (1972) and Slovak (1985) have documented the significant demand for central city spending for police registered by suburban populations; the negative correlations between wealth and community-level police strength yielded by the analysis presented here attest to the relative success of that strategy for the suburbanites who make the demands.

To locate Elyria, Columbia, and Newark in their respective state patterns, we once again turn to predictive equations derived from multiple regression analyses. Doing so by means of the same procedures followed earlier for absolute police strength yields the expectations displayed in table 3.9, which are again compared with actual scores for each city, with the differences between them expressed in terms of standard errors. Two substantive points are worth noting from these results. First, as is demonstrated in table 3.9, Elyria, Columbia, and Newark are in actuality just about where our regression equations would have predicted with regard to police visibility. Elyria's and Columbia's streets are slightly less visibly policed and Newark's are slightly more so than the predictive equations would have led us to expect, but in all three cases the emphasis is on "slightly." None is peculiar or atypical when compared with other cities or police agencies in its state, given its social and economic character. Secondly,

Table 3.9. Observed and Predicted Relative Police Strength

	Observed, 1980	Predicted, 1980	O - P Std. Error
Elyria, Ohio	1.303	1.673	− .87
Columbia, South Carolina	2.727	2.772	− .09
Newark, New Jersey	3.611	3.479	.19

these findings serve to underscore the hypothesis offered earlier about regional differences in police planning strategies and the link between those and general police styles. Here again, a regional distinction separates the agencies analyzed with regard to the attention given reported property crime rates in police planning—a nonnegligible amount in the North (in the equations for Ohio and New Jersey cities) and apparently none whatsoever in the South (in the equations for South Carolina communities). Our expectations for Elyria, Columbia, and Newark become that much more worthy of explicit attention and empirical assessment.

A Prospective Conclusion

In some ways, the empirical analyses reported in this chapter are as limited as were those reported in its predecessor. While the focus on urban communities in Ohio, South Carolina, and New Jersey brings the analysis closer to the three specific cities of interest here, it remains necessarily the case that the empirical results reported in this chapter come from community-level studies and are based on dependent variables that are, at best, only correlates of the legalistic police style. We have already noted the implications of both of these problems; suffice it to say that they hold in full force here as earlier.

Even so, these analyses have accomplished two distinct purposes. First, they have offered a general introduction to urban life and policing practice in Elyria, Columbia, and Newark; second, and more importantly, they help to flesh out at least part of the skeletal logic of inquiry that was offered at the outset of this chapter for a satisfactory study of the organization versus environment issue in the generation of police styles. Recall that that logic carried two distinct conditions. One specified a pattern of comparisons of within-city and between-city variations in police style; the second called for a pattern of correspondence between measures of style and other aspects of the urban environment and police organizational structure in each of the cities of interest. With regard to the second, the findings from the analyses presented here and in the prior chapter come together to offer predicted levels of legalistic police style against which the actual, data-based levels to be revealed by further analyses can be compared. Those predictions are summarily depicted in table 3.10.

Table 3.10. Predictors of and Predictions for the
Legalistic Police Style in Elyria, Columbia, and Newark

Predictors:	Level of Legalistic Policing Predicted, Given Value on Predictor, For		
	Elyria	*Columbia*	*Newark*
Region (North/South)	HIGH	LOW	HIGH
Urbanization (City Size, Percent Black, Crime Rates)	LOW	MODERATE	HIGH
City Manager Government	LOW	HIGH	LOW
Supervisory Span of Control in Police Agency	LOW	HIGH	HIGH
Civilianization in Police Agency	LOW	HIGH	MODERATE

The predictions presented in table 3.10 are given simple ordinal
rankings on a presumed scale of police legalism, without any mention
of the corresponding levels of either the watchmanlike or service-
oriented styles to be expected from an empirical analysis. This is
deliberate. Without more refined data on street-level police work in
the subareas of these (or any other) cities, it is difficult to say on an *a
priori* basis how levels of the different styles might or might not be
correlated with each other or with any prior organizational or environmental characteristics. Granting that, however, these predictions
about the legalistic police style are drawn in a straightforward fashion
from the narratives and the empirical results presented in this and the
preceding chapter. They can and will guide our inquiry in subsequent
chapters, where we move beyond such formal measures of local policing as relative and absolute strength and the frequency of arrests for
serious violent or property crimes, and address data that more directly
capture the essence of police styles. To that task and those data we
now turn.

Notes

1. Technically, the data on police work in Elyria and Columbia are sets of
   prerecorded materials on which secondary analysis will be conducted.
   Those from Newark were collected originally for purposes of this study.

Those data collection efforts were supported by grants from the National Science Foundation (SPI-80-28620) and the Rutgers University Research Council. The data for Elyria and Columbia were collected as parts of larger management consulting studies conducted in each city's police department by Public Administration Service, a not-for-profit research and consulting organization of which I was a member when said data were collected and said studies executed. I am grateful to Mr. George W. Greisinger, Assistant Director of Public Administration Service, for making available to me copies of those data for use in the production of this study. Needless to say, none of these agencies or organizations are responsible for the analyses or conclusions offered here or in subsequent chapters.

2. To construct these relative comparisons, Elyria's value on each of the variables was transformed into a standard normal score, or Z-score, about the statewide mean and standard deviation. This same procedure is followed for the counterpart tables for Columbia and Newark, which appear a bit later.

3. D, the index of dispersion, is calculated as:

$$D = \frac{k(N^2 - f_k^2)}{N^2(k - 1)}$$

where N is the number of cases, k the number of categories across which those cases are distributed, and f_k the frequency in each of the k categories. D varies between 0.0 and 1.0, with the latter indicating an even distribution of cases across all possible categories, and thus a very high division of labor.

4. In the mid-1970s, Columbia was estimated to be the 99th largest metropolitan market in the United States. Clearly, the presence of the military has much to do with the city's economic success and its general social structure.

5. And, as we know from victimization surveys, they understate the actual risk by factors of sizable magnitude. See U.S. Department of Justice (1976).

6. There is also the more negative argument from necessity to be offered here. Research on big-city police departments has become quite common but, excluding a few case studies, those in smaller cities like Elyria and Columbia are virtually never studied. Practically the only police measure available for secondary analysis across a broad range of American cities is that of agency size.

4. Street-Level Policing: The View from the Dispatch Log

Even lacking for the moment a definition that enjoys conceptual consensus and achieves methodological precision, the concept of a police style has basic outlines that are indeed generally recognizable. A police style, in the sense in which we discussed it in introducing this volume, is first and foremost a behavioral phenomenon. The police officers who enact a style in their work may or may not feel comfortable with it or think it an efficacious way in which to deal with citizens; but those are separate issues. The style is embodied in the officers' work, and not in their attitudes about that work. Secondly, a style is broad and encompassing. It covers the totality of what police do to, with, and for citizens and how they do it; it includes but is surely not limited to the most visible of police actions, like making arrests, conducting investigations, or issuing traffic citations. Finally, a police style is an aggregate or collective phenomenon. Individual officers enact police styles, to be sure, but they do so as members of organizations responding to environmental exigencies and sharing a common occupational culture. Police styles, in short, are sets of activities patterned by forces common to the otherwise varied individuals who engage in them.

As we have already noted, relatively little empirical research on police styles has been conducted since James Q. Wilson's (1972) seminal treatment of the topic. Of those that get closest to the concept, or that focus on substantive matters that are at least arguably closely related to it, the best have been conducted using one of two predominant methodological approaches, relying on either personal observations or personal interviews with working police officers. These can be further subcategorized by differentiating each in relatively broad terms along a structured/unstructured dimension. The studies by

Wilson (1972), Jerome Skolnick (1967) and Jonathan Rubinstein (1973) are good examples of unstructured observational studies; in each, the full range of police work is observed, recorded, and then arranged and presented by the analyst in accordance with its relevance to his or her primary scientific concerns. Structured observational studies are exemplified by the work of Donald Black (1980) and Richard Ericson (1982). Police work in the field is still the focus, but in these efforts the analyst fits the salient dimensions of that work into a more standardized data collection instrument, the results of which can be more readily subjected to quantitative analysis. Studies based on personal interviews are a half-step removed from police work in the field, in that they collect data on the occupation mediated by the accuracy of recall and the interests of interviewers and their respondents. Structured interview studies, like those of John Van Maanen (1975) or William K. Muir Jr. (1977) impose standardized questions and data collection instruments on their respondents; unstructured interviews, even when designed to tap a specific topic, will, of course, be more freewheeling and will perhaps differ from officer to officer with regard to the specific questions asked and answered (Leinen 1984; Harris 1973).

Observational studies that are supplemented by interviews (e.g., Muir 1977) are well attuned almost by their very nature to the study of two of the three general parameters of police style. In general, however, they are not well attuned to addressing the third. Solid observational research on police work focuses primarily on the actions of the officers involved, and it generally brings within view the totality of those actions. Nonetheless, it presumes as the object for study a phenomenon that is individual in character, and not aggregate. In theory, of course, a given researcher could observe all the members of one or more aggregates and cumulate the observations to attune a study to the third parameter of police style; in practice, however, this is virtually impossible for an individual researcher if the aggregates involved are at all sizable or numerous, or both. Further, unstructured observational or interview studies are nearly impossible to replicate in any serious sense of that term; their findings depend too heavily on the interests, talents, sensitivities, and shortcomings of the researchers, the entire package of which is not duplicable across analysts. In a nutshell, then, observational studies are less than optimal vehicles for systematically capturing data on police style.

The desire to uncover and ultimately to analyze differences in police styles, coupled with the practical limitations inherent in observational research, suggest that different types of data are required for empirical research in this area. Such data must recognize and tap the three general parameters of police style, and must additionally be standard or comparable across units of analysis and across researchers as well. The purpose of this chapter is to propose as a source of such data the police dispatch log, and to demonstrate the utility of using data from the log for purposes of studying street-level police action.

Data from Dispatch Logs

As a general rule, the police dispatch system comes under examination only in those—fortunately rare—instances where a citizen's request for police service is garbled in transmission or misinterpreted by the agency receiving the call, and an otherwise preventable tragedy ensues. In such an event, public attention is focused intensely but usually briefly on the dispatch system, and then usually on the adequacy of the dispatcher's training. Because these events are rare, however, the dispatch system in policing typically goes unnoticed.

This is unfortunate. In any police department that handles its own dispatching function, as do most in America, the system is a good deal more than a neutral conduit for transmitting messages from citizens to police officers. Rather, in the words of George Kelling, "The dispatch system determines the context within which the patrol officer works. That was the case in the 1960's, and continues to be so" (Kelling 1983:160).

The system's function is to receive messages about citizens' needs, to classify them into police as opposed to nonpolice matters, to transform the former into new messages consonant with the occupational dictates and practices of policing, and to transmit these transformations to officers in the field. Since a premium is usually placed on speed in the accomplishment of all this, the transformed messages sent directly to the patrol officers are little more than formalized, shorthand transmissions that cannot convey everything relevant about the situation at hand. Patrol officers, in turn, are well aware of this. They are trained in the police academy and learn further in the field how to recognize elements of the dispatched messages that convey intimations of oddity or danger in the situations they are about to encounter, and to prepare themselves accordingly. It is in this sense that, in Kelling's phrase, the "system determines the context."

Although dispatch systems vary from place to place (see, for example, the British-American comparison offered by Manning 1983), a dispatch log is almost always produced by such systems. (This is even true for police agencies that do not do their own dispatching; in such cases, the actual dispatcher will periodically provide the agency copies of dispatch records generated for its officers and its operations.) Dispatch logs are thus maintained by virtually every police agency in the country, especially by municipal police departments. They vary in technological sophistication from those generated by index cards manually completed by dispatchers during or after incidents occur to those consisting of computer tapes loaded directly by dispatchers from on-line remote terminals. Dispatch logs also vary in the detail they register about each of the incidents they include. All record the time, type, and place of the event. The more sophisticated will also record response and total service times for an incident, some indicator of the disposition of the event and, perhaps, records of prior police contacts with the address or the individuals involved in the incident. Depending on the detail and sophistication of the dispatch log, it is possible to extract a rich and precise body of data on police work in a city, in its constituent neighborhoods and, from some logs, in its specific streets and addresses. Although the analogy is not perfect, such data on police from a dispatch log are roughly similar, at an organizational level of analysis, to the time and activity budgets that researchers have gathered from participants in other working contexts.[1]

Any set of data has limitations for subsequent purposes, and the body of information typically available in police dispatch logs is no exception. Three of their specific limitations are worthy of note and comment. The first revolves around what pieces of information the logs exclude. While the incidents compiled in a police dispatch log are encounters produced by and involving individual officers or pairs of officers, any researcher interested in using dispatch material is in all likelihood collecting it toward a more aggregated level of analysis, like the neighborhood, the precinct, or perhaps the entire city. Some logs that are rich in recorded detail might allow for the tracing of events to particular households. Even so, the attitudes and values of the individual officers who participate in the recorded incidents are, of course, omitted from a dispatch log, while inferences to those from the character of the logged activities are generally precluded by the kinds of data collected for the intended aggregated analysis. In short, the talents, shortcomings, and motivations of the individual officer are almost irretrievably lost when the analysis is based on data from a dispatch log.[2]

The second limitation on such data stems from the organizational reality of their collection. Whenever events are formally recorded, a process of filtering sifts out some elements of the reality at hand while it focuses on and emphasizes others. This is only the simple phenomenology of all processes of record-keeping operated by humans. With regard to police dispatch logs, that filtering process has two separable dimensions to it. There is first the formal filtering established by organizational rules on how to record different kinds of events. It is well known that police officers and civilian police employees alike have some discretion in this regard (Ericson 1982); furthermore, departments may differ in the recording rules they impose on their members. The second dimension lies in the discretion that police have to construct accounts in such a way as to justify the actions they did or did not take in response to an incident. Within any given police agency, a sensible observer can learn these filtering rules and evaluate dispatch data accordingly, but across-agency variations in these matters might be expected to pose more severe problems for analysis.

The final problem with dispatch log information is much more pragmatic. As noted above, police logs vary in the detail and the conscientiousness with which they are kept. In agencies where record-keeping is not a priority and hence is monitored only in a very spotty fashion, the log will contain a number of unfillable gaps. Further, the simpler systems will merely fail to record materials relevant to and important for empirical analysis. In short, data quality within a police department may or may not be high, depending on the priority attached to record-keeping and maintenance; availability of data across agencies can thus be equally problematic.

These limitations are admittedly matters for some concern to any researcher, but they do not disqualify the use of such materials for research purposes. The first certainly precludes individual-level studies, but it poses no problem for efforts at more aggregated levels of analysis. It precludes analysis of the workers, but not that of the settings in which or the patterns by which the work itself is conducted. In a similar vein, the third problem poses limits at both the departmental and the comparative level on what kinds of questions might be asked, but it does not eliminate the asking of questions altogether.

The phenomenological issue is obviously the most critical, for it is the one that must be resolved if the data collected from dispatch logs are to support valid and reliable empirical research. Fortunately, in regard to both these issues—validity and reliability—evidence of various types is available to suggest that data from dispatch logs meet the standards for a satisfactory resolution of both, and that the logs themselves are thus a solid source of data for secondary analysis in police research. Their validity is reinforced by the structure of the situation in which they are created. Unlike the arrest reports or contact cards manufactured by police officers after their encounters with citizens, dispatch records are generally collected before a police–citizen contact. Almost all of the entries in dispatch logs are gathered directly in telephone calls from citizens to the dispatcher, who must then pass along the relevant pieces of information from those calls to a patrol officer or unit. Since most American police departments place a premium on speed of dispatch and officer response[3] there is little time available to a dispatcher who might seek to manipulate a logged entry. Further, there is little interest on anyone's part in having him or her do so. Neither court action nor departmental review are typically based in any serious way on dispatch log data; arrest reports, contact cards, interrogation reports and the many other "final reports" that are a regular part of contemporary policing are the primary sources for subsequent evaluations by departmental insiders and outsiders alike. In effect, then, dispatch logs contain a mass of data which are used to spur police action but in the collection of which there is generally neither the time nor the interest necessary to motivate their manipulation. By virtue of this, dispatch log data are arguably more valid sources of information on police work than are any other records kept in American police departments.[4]

Empirical research on the general validity of the gamut of entries contained in police logs is virtually nonexistent, but a few scholars have addressed specific types of log entries to compare frequencies of the events recorded in them with frequencies derived from other nonlog and even nonpolice sources. The most recent effort of this type is that of Berk and Newton (1985), who were interested in the effects of arrest on subsequent instances of spouse abuse. They report that in their study site, a cross-checking of interview data gathered directly from abuse victims yielded recidivism counts not significantly different from those recorded in logs and other police departmental record sources. Such findings lend further credence to the contention of validity for dispatch log data.

The reliability of the data extractable from police logs should also be relatively strong across police agencies, although here again the evidence must come from an assessment of the structure of the situation in which dispatching is carried out, because empirical research on the matter is lacking. Nonetheless, it is worth noting that the dispatch function is generally invariant across police departments in the United States with regard to the time and speed constraints discussed above; the premium placed on direct recording of data and its speedy transmission to a patrol unit is well nigh universal in this country. Further, the formal data-recording rules followed by dispatchers in any police department are learnable; in fact, they are usually themselves matters of formal procedural record and such records can be systematically compared and adjusted for interagency differences in procedure. The more informal variations on these recording rules adopted by dispatchers and officers to meet unforeseen local situations and operational needs are also learnable, with sufficient observation, which suggests that dispatch procedures and the logs that result from them can be made to be reasonably comparable across agencies. The development of American policing as an occupation in turn suggests that the adjustments required are neither extensive nor onerous. Police agencies and executives in America regularly share information, procedures, and successful resolutions of problems in the meetings of professional associations at the national, state, and metropolitan levels. The occupational publications of those groups further contribute to information dissemination and innovation diffusion in policing. Procedures and technologies for dispatching and data storage and retrieval are topics regularly treated in these meetings and publications. Further, during the police professionalization movement of the 1970s (Caiden 1977), technical assistance and consultation in various policing functions—among them dispatching—was widely and readily provided to municipal police departments by the U.S. Law Enforcement Assistance Administration. Companies that manufacture and market dispatching technologies continue to offer those same services, albeit for a price. Because of all of these aspects of occupational development and information diffusion, the data collected and stored in police dispatch logs and the processes underlying their collection and storage approach a commonality across agencies, thanks to the common needs they seek to meet and the common interests of the profession as a whole in filling those. As a result, the data collected in such logs generally are, or can easily be made to be, substantively comparable.

Measures for This Study:
Definitions, Samples, and Comparative Availability

The data on police work and neighborhood-level police styles in Elyria, Columbia, and Newark were drawn from the dispatch logs maintained by their respective police departments. In Elyria, the production process for the dispatch log is completely manual. The dispatcher completes a multiple-copy incident record form as notification of each event is received from a citizen and as each event is handled by an officer; a copy of each form is forwarded to the central filing room, where it and the other daily records of local police action are retained in an easily accessible cabinet. In Columbia, small forms recording the salient details of incidents are completed by the dispatchers as the incidents occur; later, those details are keypunched from the forms and read into the municipal computer, from which incident reports are produced for the police department. In Newark, the dispatch system is fully computerized. Information is entered into storage in an on-line system as soon as the details of an incident become known. The information is stored permanently on electronic tape, and tapes for a number of past years are readily available.

At the close of the 1970s, the Elyria Police Department was handling roughly 25,000 service incidents per year; Columbia, about 120,000; Newark, nearly 200,000. To gather data for this study, a sampling procedure was employed in each research site to extract a more manageable number of cases. The sampling plans differed somewhat across the three police departments, with the differences stemming from two sources: data availability and the size of their respective universes of police calls. The data on Elyria derive from a systematic sample of all calls received by the Elyria police over the year before data collection, a period stemming from approximately July 1, 1978 through June 30, 1979. The sampling ratio used was .1; data were recorded for every tenth logged incident. An alternative procedure using a sample of days would have been problematic in the Elyria case primarily because the likelihood of misfiling incident forms for any given day is probably nonnegligible in a manual recording and storage system. Since the number of incidents handled per day by the Elyria police is not particularly large, such misfiling could result in a markedly biased collection of data. By way of contrast, the data from Columbia do not technically constitute a sample; rather, they derive from the universe of all calls received by the Columbia Police Department during the 28-day period from July 1 through July 28, 1979. This rather severe limitation on data collection in Columbia was necessitated by the fact that at the time the data were gathered, Columbia's computer facilities for sampling from a large data base were nonexistent. That particular month was the most recent one for which the available data had been completely logged and transferred to the municipal computer. Finally, the data on police work in Newark represent the universe of events occurring during the year between March 1, 1980 and February 28, 1981. For data collection in Newark, a random sample of twenty days was drawn from the relevant year, and data were collected on all of the incidents which occurred during each of those days.[5]

But for the difference of two years between the period during which they were collected, the data from Elyria and Newark are in general terms relatively comparable. Both sets of data span a year of time and both include the natural variations in police work stemming from time of the day, day of the week, and season of the year. This is particularly true of the Elyria data, coming from a systematic sample. The raw data gathered for Newark represent a slight undersampling of Saturdays and Sundays and a slight oversampling of Wednesdays, for which compensation was made by weighting the data on the basis of these disproportions. The Columbia data are not so general with regard to the time period they cover. They capture hourly and daily variations in police work sufficiently well, and they neither over- nor under-sample specific days; but they are collected for only a summer season. This is, of course, a period of relatively high demand for police services, which means that the relative frequency of police calls in Columbia is inflated in these data by means of the sampling procedure employed. Note, however, that a general analysis of Columbia Police Department annual reports suggests that this summertime inflation is not specific to particular types of police work; rather, it seems a general inflation cutting across everything the police do. Hence, a simple deflation weighting[6] applied to the Columbia data makes them reasonably representative of a year's worth of logged events.

The various weighting procedures applied to these data and the purposes behind their application are summarized in table 4.1. To make dispatch log data amenable to analysis within a given city, the cases analyzed must reliably capture variations in police action for a representative period of time. This is naturally accomplished in the sampling procedures for Elyria and Columbia; it is produced in Newark by weighting for under- or over-sampled days. To make the data amenable to comparative analysis across the cities, the representative time period measured must be of a fixed and equal length. In

Table 4.1. Weighting Procedures

	Goal:	
City	*Comparability of Data for Analyzing Internal Variations in Police Work*	*Comparability of Data for Analyzing Variations in Police Work Across Cities*
Elyria, Ohio	Achieved in Original Sampling Procedure	Achieved by Multiplying Cases by 10
Columbia, South Carolina	Achieved in Original Sampling Procedure	Achieved by Multiplying Cases by 13.04 and Deflating Total by 10%
Newark, New Jersey	Achieved by Weighting for Disproportionately Sampled Days	Achieved by Multiplying Cases by 17.44

this study, a 365-day year stands as the standard; comparability across cities is achieved by multiplying the cases collected in each by the factor of 365 which their respective representative time periods constitute and, in Columbia, by then applying the required seasonal deflator.

In general, two types of measures were sought from the data collected for Elyria, Columbia, and Newark: measures tapping actual dimensions of police action with regard to the incident in question, and measures tapping the context within which that action occurred. Initial data collection plans called for the gathering of information on twelve variables, six of the action variety and six on context. The six measures of context were: (1) the day of the incident; (2) the time of day when it occurred; (3) whether the incident occurred on a weekend; (4) the type of incident; (5) the relative priority allotted to it by the police department in question; and (6) the geographical area of the city.

Day and time measures are straightforward, and need no elaboration here.[7] Weekend occurrences were defined as 6 P.M. Friday through 6 A.M. Monday. The priority measure is not a matter of our imposition of a normative standard on otherwise neutral data; rather it is the relative seriousness attached to an event by the police department in question. Such priority rankings are clearly allocational devices by means of which a police department attempts to rationalize the deployment of its officers and equipment. Incident types are those summary descriptions of the nature of an incident defined by each of the police departments, usually by the dispatchers who first receive knowledge of an incident and who then allot it a priority ranking to guide their attempt to dispatch officers to the scene. Finally, area refers to that geographic subdivision of the city in which the incident of interest occurred. As recorded in the dispatch logs, these are generally the patrol beats, precincts, or districts by means of which local police work is territorially organized.

Six measures of the nature of police action were sought in the data collected for each of the three cities of interest here: (1) source of initiation of police action; (2) response time, (3) service time expended in handling an incident; (4) formalization of an incident; (5) substantive disposition of an incident; and (6) style.

Many of these have appeared in other studies of American police, albeit occasionally under somewhat different names. Source of initiation refers to whether an event was brought to the attention of the police through the efforts of a citizen or a police officer. It taps the proactive-reactive dimension of police work first identified by Bordua and Reiss (1967) and subsequently made critical to the now famous Kansas City Preventive Patrol Experiment (Kelling et al. 1974). Response time is defined as the time elapsed between receipt of notice of an incident by the police and the arrival of an officer on the scene; similarly, service time is the elapsed time between receipt of information and the patrol officer's report that the incident has been cleared. Both have appeared in studies of police patrol allocation (Larsen 1972). Formalization distinguishes between events that required the police officer to make a formal report from those that did not. Given the importance of secrecy in police work (Manning 1974, 1978), formalization as defined here is an important indicator of what becomes "common knowledge" to the police in a community. Substantive disposition refers to the actual nature of the way in which an officer concludes a police incident: making an arrest, adjudicating a dispute, or doing nothing. As Black (1970) has shown, dispositions vary markedly with the nature of an event and the demands of the citizens most immediately involved in it. Finally, police style is envisioned as a measure to be derived from those already discussed. Specific measurement procedures with regard to it will be discussed in detail in chapter 5.

Of the context and activity measures that were sought for this analysis, most—but not all—were available in the police dispatch logs. Table 4.2 summarizes the situation on data availability by noting what raw measures were available in and collected from each city's police log (the top part) and what measures were derivable from those figures (the bottom part) in each study site. The twelve specific measures noted previously as the primary subjects of the analytical focus of this study are indicated in the table by asterisks.

Of the three collections of data on police work gathered for this research, that for Columbia is without the doubt the spottiest. Only eight items of information were available about and thus collected on police calls in Columbia, namely: (1) day of occurrence; (2) type of call; (3) neighborhood of occurrence; (4) time of day at which the call was received by the police; (5) time of day at which the call was

Table 4.2. Comparative Data Availability

	Elyria, Ohio	Columbia, South Carolina	Newark, New Jersey
I. Measures Available in the Raw Data			
*Day of Occurrence	x	x	x
*Time of Occurrence/ Receipt of Call	x	x	x
Time of Dispatch of Call		x	
Time of Officer Arrival		x	x
Time of Call Clearance		x	x
*Type of Call	x	x	x
*Priority of Call			x
*Initiation of Call	x	x	x
*Neighborhood/Precinct of Occurrence	x	x	x
Disposition:			
*Formalization	x		x
*Substantive Type			x
II. Measures Created by Data Transformations			
*Weekend Occurrence	x	x	x
*Style of Police Work	x	x	x
*Response Time		x	x
*Total Service Time		x	x

dispatched; (6) time of day at which an officer arrived on the scene to handle the call; (7) time of day at which the call was reported cleared (or completed) by the officer on the scene; and (8) source of initiation of the call (an officer or a citizen).

From these data, nine of the desired police activity and context measures can be derived. Note, however, that the material on incident types was precoded in Columbia—before I obtained access to it—into five broad categories of calls: crime (part I), crime (part II), traffic, service, and administrative. These are less than auspicious labels, because they combine far too many different kinds of specific incidents under their general headings. For example, "part II crimes" includes all relatively nonserious breaches of the criminal law (like malicious mischief, possession of marijuana, and disorderly conduct) as well as those disputes among citizens that are not themselves violations (like family fights or neighbor disputes) but could become such under certain circumstances. The procedural routines used for creating these broad categories in Columbia are available, so comparable categories can be created for the police data in the other two cities. Nonetheless, the Columbia data cannot be further disaggregated with regard to type of event. This is a distinct disadvantage to using these data. Note, further, that no data whatsoever from Columbia are available with regard to the disposition of calls, which is another serious shortcoming. All things considered, the data from Columbia are the weakest of the three data sets.

The data collected from Elyria are of moderately greater richness than are those from Columbia. For Elyria, the following data elements on police calls were collected: (1) day of occurrence; (2) type of call; (3) neighborhood of occurrence; (4) time of day at which the call was received; (5) source of initiation of the call (an officer or a citizen); and (6) disposition (formalization).

Compared with Columbia, Elyria provides two fewer data elements and one fewer measure of the twelve desired but, on the whole, a good deal more information. Not only do the Elyria data specify whether any given logged incident concluded formally (i.e., by the making of an arrest or the taking of a formal report), but they also record a good deal more about the substantive nature of those calls, for the Elyria Police Department codes the requests for service it receives into one of more than fifty event categories. In this regard, where Columbia provided too little information, Elyria is closer to the other extreme. Fifty categories are too many for analytic purposes, so some will have to be collapsed into larger, more general groupings. With the Elyria data, however, we can control that process, which is a situation far superior to that encountered with the Columbia material, where we cannot exercise such control. What we cannot do in Elyria that we can in Columbia is build measures of response or total service time required for a given call.

From Newark comes both our largest and our richest set of data. Ten data elements were recorded on police calls from the files of the Newark Police Department, namely: (1) day of occurrence; (2) type of call; (3) priority of the call, according to department policy; (4) neighborhood of occurrence; (5) time of day at which the call was received; (6) time of day at which an officer arrived on the scene; (7) time at which the call was reported cleared; (8) source of initiation of the call (an officer or a citizen); (9) disposition of the call; and (10) whether that disposition was formal or not.

The Newark Police Department uses a 139-category scheme for recording the type of call received, and these data preserve the exact category recorded for an incident. Again, this is a relative embarrassment of riches, but it gives us considerable control over the recategorization of incident types into more general categories. Similarly, the department's coding scheme for dispositions is 37 categories long, and these data reproduce all the alternative categories. Note that this one measure is sufficiently detailed to record not only whether an event was formalized by means of the taking of a report, but also the specific substantive character of the disposition itself. From all these pieces of information, all twelve of the desired variables for this analysis can be measured. As a result, the dispatch log data from Newark offers us the best of all possible worlds: the detail on time available in Columbia as well as that on the nature and outcome of calls available in Elyria. With regard to the latter, however, the Newark data go a good deal further.

Data Quality

The processes of information receipt, recording, and storage that characterize the police dispatch systems in Elyria, Columbia, and Newark vary considerably in their respective degrees of computerization and sophistication. They vary as well in the quantity of data that they record. Further, the covariation along both these dimensions would appear to be straightforward and monotonic: the more sophisticated the system, the more data it records. The quality of the data available in each of these police logs varies as well, albeit not monotonically with either sophistication or data availability. In general, however, data quality across all three logs is relatively high.

Table 4.3 provides the relevant detail on comparative data quality, by listing for all the recorded and derived measures of police activity and context of the event the percentage of cases from each log for

Table 4.3. Comparative Data Quality

Measures:	Elyria, Ohio		Columbia, South Carolina		Newark, New Jersey	
	(1)	(2)	(1)	(2)	(1)	(2)
*Day of Week	100.0	100.0	100.0	100.0	100.0	100.0
*Time of Occurrence	99.7	99.5	99.0	99.1	99.8	99.8
Time Dispatched	—	—	76.2	83.0	—	98.2
Time Police Arrived	—	—	60.2	65.9	98.2	98.5
Time Incident Cleared	—	—	71.7	74.8	98.4	98.5
*Priority of Incident	—	—	—	—	99.3	99.9
*Type of Incident	99.9	99.9	96.3	95.1	99.3	99.9
*Initiation Source	99.8	99.9	60.3	65.3	98.2	98.2
*Neighborhood of Occurrence	89.5	92.1	69.9	75.3	86.1	88.1
Disposition:						
*Formalization	99.7	99.8	—	—	97.7	98.1
*Substance	—	—	—	—	97.7	98.1
*Occurrence on Weekend	99.7	99.5	99.1	99.1	99.8	99.8
*Response Time	—	—	59.6	65.9	98.2	98.2
*Service Time	—	—	70.3	74.8	98.5	98.5
*Service-Delivery Style	99.8	99.9	60.3	65.9	97.7	98.2
N of Cases	2674	2492	9464	7181	11509	10822

which measures are actually available. Dashes in the table indicate measures not recorded in one or more of the logs. The table also includes the number of cases in each dispatch log sample on which these percentages are based. Note that for each study site, two columns of percentages are presented in table 4.3: those based on total samples of cases, and those based on truncated samples which exclude events of a purely administrative nature, involving no contacts with citizens. While such administrative matters are indeed a part of police work, they are largely irrelevant to the matter of police style and the issue of its determination, and can thus be safely eliminated from the analysis.

Elyria and Newark provide us with particularly strong data sets. With one exception in each city—that of "neighborhood of occurrence"—none of the measures registers a proportion of missing data greater than 2.5% of the original sample, and on most that percentage actually drops under 2.0%. Even for the neighborhood measures, where missing values characterize 10 to 15% of the cases, there is no need for any alarm for a disproportionate number of these problem cases are administrative matters and not police–citizen encounters. Based on the samples of calls for nonadministrative police services, the data for both Elyria and Newark constitute virtually complete records of police work for the periods in question.

The story is a bit different with regard to the data for Columbia. As the table demonstrates, those data have some notable gaps, particularly with regard to response times and sources of the initiation of the incident. In part, these gaps are artifacts of the inclusion of administrative cases in the overall sample; fully 25% of all of the logged incidents in the Columbia log are administrative, of which in turn better than half have no indicator of source of initiation. (It was almost always a police officer or administrator.) These facts alone cause the quality percentages for the cases of substantive importance in Columbia to rise notably above those depicted for the total sample. Nonetheless, it remains true that Columbia provides the weakest set of police dispatch data for this study, in terms of data quality.

Excursus: An Additional Hypothesis on the Legalistic Police Style

The empirical analyses of police strength levels and urban arrets rates reported in the preceding chapters yielded a set of hypotheses about the city-level and police-agency-level determinants of the legalistic police style. Those hypotheses were summarized at the close of chapter 3. From the description of the technologies and processes underlying the police dispatch systems in Elyria, Columbia, and Newark, another such hypothesis can now be culled.

As was noted above, the information recording systems in the police departments in Elyria, Columbia, and Newark vary widely in terms of mechanization, with Elyria's system falling toward the primitive end of the continuum, Newark's toward the advanced end, and Columbia's in-between. As was also noted, there appears to be a monotonic, positive relationship between mechanization and the quantity of information a system stores. At best, however, a curvilinear relationship between mechanization and data quality seems to emerge, such that both the least and the most mechanized systems provide data of uniformly high quality while the moderately mechanized system falls notably behind in this regard. That the former relationship should hold seems unsurprising; that the latter should hold as well deserves further comment.

Mechanization of the processes of information storage and retrieval in a police department—or for that matter in any type of formal organization—is not simply a matter of substituting machines for humans. In fact, it is far more akin to the interactive social process wherein an innovation is introduced into an ongoing social system. What becomes necessary in the face of the introduction of such an innovation is what Janowitz (1969, 1976) has called the process of institution-building. A substantial amount of social learning must occur, accompanied perhaps by a certain readjustment in the structure of the system, before the innovation will be completely adopted, the larger system will be reintegrated around that innovation, and the increased productivity projected to occur as a result will be manifested. In the early stages of that process, it is not at all unlikely to see productivity fall rather than rise; in such a context, the level of preinnovation productivity is interrupted by the innovation, while the necessary social learning and system adaptation have not had time to work themselves out. That appears to be the case with regard to the police dispatch systems in Elyria, Columbia, and Newark. In Elyria and in Newark, information availability varies with mechanization as one might expect, but information quality is uniformly high, suggesting a

· high level of adaptation to the records systems extant in each. The moderate level of data availability in moderately mechanized Columbia, when coupled to the comparatively low level of data quality, suggests an organization that has not yet completely undergone the learning and adaptation functions attendant on the adoption of an innovation.

Is there a carryover between stage in the process of institution-building with regard to police information systems and levels or styles of police performance? We cannot answer that question with any precision or confidence; the research required to do so is generally non-existent. Law enforcement professionals, however, have argued that such a connection does exist. One of the last major experiments in police performance that the Law Enforcement Assistance Administration sponsored prior to its demise was the Integrated Criminal Apprehension Program (ICAP). The program was specifically designed to upgrade police information storage and retrieval systems in order to make feasible the conduct of crime analysis at a relatively sophisticated level. It was further intended to more closely integrate the conduct of such analyses with strategies for police patrol planning and manpower allocations, with improvements in the latter hypothesized to result in higher rates of criminal apprehension. In general, ICAP was planned and carried out on the assumption that levels of police data quality and availability were positively, if indirectly, correlated with levels of police performance in making criminal arrests.

Now, aggressive police work aimed at apprehending criminals is in many respects a good description of the legalistic police style, which is oriented to the dictates of the formal criminal law and is characterized by a high level of police initiation of law-enforcement-related events based on the availability and use of sophisticated bodies of information. If the ICAP hypothesis is generally accurate as a model of reality, then its projected pattern of results with regard to information systems and police action should emerge in Elyria, Columbia, and Newark. Compared to each other, Newark should be a relatively legalistic police agency, more proactively attuned to law enforcement events and more formalistic in its treatment of dispatch incidents, while Elyria should be somewhat less so. Columbia should occupy, at best, a position near Elyria in this regard; however, given the results on data quality depicted earlier in table 4.3, it should probably realistically be expected to register the lowest score of the three on the relative predominance of police legalism. This, in turn, constitutes another hypothesis that can be added to the set detailed at the close of chapter 3 and can serve to guide the analyses to be presented in subsequent chapters.

Street-Level Policing: The View from the Log

What kind of a picture of the substance of police work emerges from the entries recorded in a dispatch log? The remainder of this chapter seeks to answer that question by means of a serial description of the major contextual patterns in police activity that are captured in the data gathered from the police logs in Elyria, Columbia and Newark. In providing an answer to that question, this presentation seeks further to lay the groundwork for the more rigorous analysis of the determinants and dimensions of police style, the task taken up in the subsequent chapters of this volume.

The expositions that follow are city-specific, so as to avoid the analytic problem posed by the availability of different measures in different research sites. Granting this, however, the descriptions of policing offered here are conceptually linked; all are informed by a situational perspective on police work. In broad terms, that perspective suggests that context structures action; more specifically, it suggests that what police do in any given encounter with citizens is a function of the temporal, substantive, and territorial contexts within which the encounter occurs. The descriptions that follow are linked in that each, within the limits of the data available to it, seeks to uncover the degree to which that is so.[8]

Elyria, Ohio The simple passage of time seems, at first glance, a relatively trivial matter to include in an analysis of police work. As a gross counting of hours or minutes, it probably is; as a sociocultural reality, however, it takes on a good deal more significance. Most social activities are structured around the passage of time in such a way as to make the social order both quantitatively and qualitatively a different phenomenon around blocks of that passage. This becomes clear when we focus on the idea of a "social order" as a patterned set of interactions structured reflexively by the participants involved in it. Now consider the social order of the neighborhood or local community of residence. Most contemporary Americans are completely unconscious of that order or of threats posed to it late at night. Further, those who work away from their homes generally lose consciousness of that local social order and focus more on their work-related orders during business hours. Most people are thus available to participate in the neighborhood social order and to serve as agents of informal control over it only when they are not at work. In that police respond not only to citizens' calls but also to their on-the-scene demands (Black 1970; Black and Reiss 1970), we might well expect that the patterns of local police work would vary with the passage of time.[9]

There is indeed a temporal dimension to the sheer quantity of police work recorded in the Elyria dispatch log. Fridays and Saturdays account for a modest disproportion of the sampled police events (32.5% of the sampled events; 28.6% of the time in a typical week) as do the periods more formally defined as weekends (37.5% of the events; 35.7% of the time). Both of these pairs of differences are in the direction anticipated by our discussion of the temporal basis of local social life. That the latter is smaller than the former is accounted for, in these data, by the fact that Sunday is a disproportionately "slow" day for the Elyria police.[10]

Similar variations emerge when the focus turns to specific hours of the typical day. Were police action a random phenomenon, any given hour of the day would be expected to account for about 4.3% of all police events. Police action obviously is not random; nonetheless, this

Table 4.4. Event Initiation and Formalization in Elyria

Source of Initiation:	Formalization	
	No	Yes
Police Officer	22.7%	77.3%
	(76)	(259)
Citizen	61.4%	38.6%
	(1322)	(831)
Total	56.2%	43.8%
	(1398)	(1090)

Yule's Q = − .69

standard is not so artificial as it might seem at first glance. Police officers can initiate activity, as well as simply respond to it. Presuming that police are not particularly enamored of doing nothing during a tour of duty, they might be expected to attempt to fill "dead time" by initiating events, and thus more or less even out the temporal variations in their workloads. In Elyria, however, police workloads are not evened out over any given day. The hours of 8 A.M. to 9 A.M., 11 A.M. to noon, 1 P.M. to 2 P.M., 4 P.M. to 6 P.M., and 8 P.M. to 2 A.M. account for disproportionately large numbers of police events when compared with the random expectation.

Of more interest than the temporal pattern to the level of police activity in Elyria is the temporal pattern of its character, specifically the temporal dimensions of police initiation and formalization of events. In Elyria, there is a strong link between the two, as displayed in table 4.4: although they are rare on an absolute basis, police-initiated events are far more likely to be formalized than are citizen-initiated ones. Further, each has something of a temporal dimension as well. Police initiation of an event is significantly[11] more likely if that event comes on a weekend and between the hours of 11 P.M. and 6 A.M. Police formalization of an event, however, is another matter. Events are significantly more likely to be formalized if they fall on a Sunday, Monday, Tuesday, or Wednesday and between the hours of 10 A.M. and 6 P.M.

There is something of an anomaly in these results. As we have seen, when the police in Elyria are proactive, they tend to formalize the events they encounter and handle. On any given day, the Elyria police tend to become slightly more proactive as the general citizenry withdraws from active involvement in the neighborhood social order. However, the police are relatively more proactive on weekends, even though citizens are more available. Nonetheless, formalization by police does not correspond to these temporal patterns; rather, it tends to occur early in the work week and primarily during working hours. Part of the resolution of this paradox might plausibly lie in the other contexts, geographic or substantive, that condition police work in Elyria.

In recording incidents in their dispatch log, the Elyria police use a list of more than 50 different categories to identify the substantive nature of the nonadministrative incidents they handle. Figure 4.1 displays those incident types in accordance with their respective like-

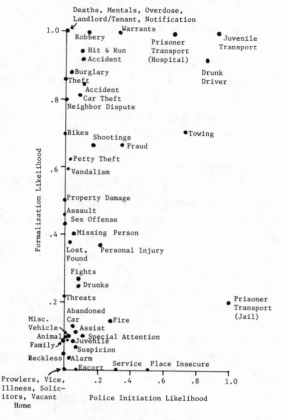

Figure 4.1. Event Analysis for Elyria, Ohio

lihoods of being police-initiated and formalized. It is clear that some types of calls are never formalized. These include "city services," "escorts," checks on vacant homes or complaints about solicitors and salespeople. These constitute what the Elyria police see as the minutiae of local police work. At the opposite extreme, some calls are always or almost always formalized by means of a written report. Those include "deaths," the transportation of juveniles or suspects taken into custody, the serving of warrants, subpoenas, or official notifications, and the handling of robbery reports. To some extent, the same kind of variation occurs when we consider the calls that are most likely to be initiated by police officers. Some types—such as prisoner or juvenile transportation or the handling of drunk drivers—are nearly always initiated by police. Far and away, however, most kinds of calls are initiated by the citizen, from the most petty (like dog complaints) to the most serious (like robbery or assault). As in most other American cities, police work in Elyria is primarily reactive work.

Categories of events that are typically police-initiated in Elyria are relatively few, but the formalization rates for those same categories are relatively high. That is not particularly surprising, since most of those events involve taking people or property into custody. Here, of course, the rights of the involved persons or property owners are heavy, and police liability for misfeasance or malfeasance becomes a weighty consideration. Formalization in this context protects the officers against such charges. For categories of events that are usually citizen-initiated, however, the variety of formalization is broad. What seems most interesting in this regard is that incidents involving property are likely to be formalized while those involving only persons are not. Splitting the formalization axis in figure 4.1 at .5 divides the event categories on a 20:26 ratio. Of the 20 types most frequently formalized, at least 11 (55%) involve property damaged, disputed, or stolen. Of the 26 relatively nonformalized types, only 6 (21%) involve similar matters. In Elyria, what happens to property is far more likely than what happens to people to become a formal police event.

Since the different types of events vary widely in the frequency with which they occur, they cannot by themselves account for the anomaly noted above about the temporal dimensions of policing in Elyria. They do, however, offer a clue to its resolution. Figure 4.1 suggests that what the police initiate they formalize, but that what they formalize they have not necessarily initiated. We also noted from the figure the apparent centrality of disputes over property to the outcome of formalization in citizen-initiated events. If these disputes are disproportionately Sunday through Wednesday affairs, while the police-initiated events are evening or weekend matters, the paradox will be resolved.

Among the events sampled from the Elyria police log, there are 335 police-initiated nonadministrative matters. Of these, 215 (64.1%) come from prisoner transportation, drunk driver apprehensions, or vehicle towing; of these 215 incidents, 112 (52.1%) occur on weekends. Hence, the few types of events that the police tend to *both* initiate and formalize tend to occur on weekends, which resolves half of the paradox. The other half is likewise resolved, once we collapse incident varieties along a property/nonproperty dichotomy. Between Sundays and Wednesdays, 35.9% of the incidents handled are property-related; the corresponding percentage for Thursdays through Saturdays is 33.3. By the same token, the events occurring during that portion of any given day falling between 10 A.M. and 6 P.M. are property-related affairs 40.1% of the time; the corresponding percentage for the remaining hours is 31.6. As we surmised above, property matters—which are not very likely to be police-initiated but are highly likely to be formalized—are themselves structured by temporal variations. As a result, so is the character of police action.

Another way to reduce the complexity of the Elyria data on incident type is to recode the sampled events into one of the four general substantive categories with which police officials most frequently deal: serious crimes (Part I offenses according to the FBI Uniform Crime Reporting System), less serious crimes and disputes (Part II offenses), non-law-enforcement services, and traffic events. Such a coding scheme is a relatively formal affair that masks some important variations among the specific types of events that it groups together. We make use of it here nonetheless because it is commonly used by police and in order to build the basis for a later comparison with Columbia, where such a coding scheme is the only one available for the sampled events. Table 4.5 displays the frequency distribution of sampled events in Elyria in accordance with this scheme. Further, it portrays the percentages of such events that are officer-initiated and formalized, and the associated test statistics and measures of association yielded by the full contingency tables including each of these measures.

Until we can look at similar results for Columbia and Newark, and until we can develop a formal measure of police styles, it is a bit risky to give police work in Elyria a definitive label as either service-oriented, legalistic, or watchmanlike. Table 4.5 does hint, however, that the last of these may be the most appropriate and accurate designation. The Elyria police are more frequently involved in disputes, disorders and less serious criminal events than in any other types of incidents, but these involvements are most likely to be reactive and to end informally. On the surface, at least, that sounds like a watchmanlike police agency. For the moment, however, what seems most notable from table 4.5 is the magnitude of the relationship between event type and each of the two dimensions of police activity available in these data. These magnitudes are indexed by the values of Cramer's V displayed in the table. On an absolute scale, these values are nonnegligible; police initiation and event formalization, and especially the

Table 4.5. Event Type and Police Action in Elyria

Event Types:	Relative Frequency	Percent of Events That	
		Are Police-Initiated	Are Formalized
Serious Crimes	11.3%	3.9%	72.8%
Less Serious Crimes and Disputes	38.1%	6.4%	25.4%
Traffic Calls	34.0%	25.4%	69.1%
Service Calls	16.7%	11.6%	15.0%
χ^2	—	167.42	584.68
P	—	.001	.001
Cramer's V	—	.26	.48

latter, respond to the substantive definitions that police impose on the requests for service they receive. On a more relative scale, these co-efficients are even more impressive; both substantially exceed the values of the same indicators computed to tap the time-proactivity (Cramer's $V = .07$) and time-formalization (Cramer's $V = .11$) relationships depicted above. For the moment, substantive type emerges rather clearly as the stronger causal agent in patterning the nature of police action in Elyria.

Assessing the neighborhood context of police work in Elyria—and for that matter in Columbia and Newark as well—poses a bit of a problem, for there is no commonly accepted definition of a "neighborhood" by means of which to differentiate a city into a set of standard component parts that are amenable to further analysis. For police patrol purposes, Elyria is divided into three general districts or beats to which officers are assigned, but the assignments vary from officer to officer on almost a daily basis and the number and boundaries of the beats occasionally vary as well, as circumstances dictate. As a matter of standard procedure, police dispatchers collect the specific addresses at which incidents occur, but these are not later recoded into neighborhood-level categories.[12] Elyria's city planners divide the city into a set of 28 neighborhoods, the boundaries of which are relatively fixed; unfortunately, relatively little original information is collected for the neighborhoods so defined. Furthermore, the boundaries of the neighborhoods and of the police beats generally do not coincide.

To assess the differential effects of organization and neighborhood

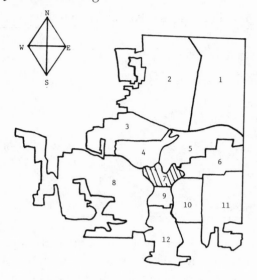

Note: Source Map - 1970 U.S. Census

Figure 4.2. Constructed Neighborhoods for Elyria, Ohio

in the patterning of police activities and the generation of police
styles, it is necessary to collect measures of the social, demographic,
and economic characteristics of the neighborhoods in which police
work is conducted, as well as measures of the work itself. The best
source of such material is, of course, the U.S. Census. In 1970, the
Census Bureau divided Elyria into 13 census tracts, only some of
which corresponded with the neighborhoods defined by the city planners. This problem of conflicting boundaries is not specific to Elyria; a
similar version occurs in Columbia and Newark as well. In Elyria, it
was resolved by aggregating planners' neighborhoods toward census
tracts until boundary convergence appeared satisfactory on the basis
of visual inspection. In a few instances, aggregations of neighborhoods
perfectly matched aggregations of tracts; just as often, however, they
did not. While mismatches did not involve much physical territory—to
be precise, never more than ten city blocks—they did nonetheless
exist. Figure 4.2 maps the resulting aggregates, and thus offers a
pictorial orientation for the data analyses that follow in this and the
subsequent chapters. Area 7 in that figure contains the bulk of Elyria's
central business district; the others are primarily, albeit not totally,
residential in character. Table 4.6 displays the frequency distributions

Table 4.6. Neighborhoods and Police Action in Elyria

Areas:	Relative Frequency	Proportion of Calls That Are	
		Police-Initiated	Formalized
1	8.0	9.8	41.3
2	8.8	10.4	45.5
3	7.3	10.7	39.3
4	9.8	11.2	42.9
5	6.1	10.7	44.3
6	7.5	9.4	45.1
7	13.4	26.0	51.8
8	6.9	15.8	44.9
9	6.3	9.0	44.8
10	9.0	6.8	38.6
11	8.7	12.0	42.0
12	8.1	8.6	37.1
χ^2	—	68.43	18.17
P	—	.001	.058
Cramer's V	—	.17	.09

of calls received by these aggregated areas, and the proportions of calls in each that are police-initiated and formalized. Again, indicators of the area-action association and results of significance tests for the relevant full contingency tables are also included.

Territorial context does relatively little to structure the nature of local police action in Elyria. While the 12 neighborhoods are hardly carbon copies of each other, neither do they vary to any sizable degree with regard to police proactivity or police event formalization. This is particularly true for the latter, where the distribution by neighborhood fails even to attain statistical significance. Proactivity fares better, but the general area-initiation association is nonetheless a modest one (Cramer's V = .17). It would shrink even further, probably to statistical insignificance, were it not for the particularly high levels of police initiation of events characteristic of the business district (area 7), with relatively few residents. Here, and apparently only here, is proactive policing in Elyria something out of the ordinary.

The magnitude of the area-action association in Elyria is, for all practical purposes, no stronger than that of the time-action relationship, and both are dwarfed by the effects of incident type. That the latter is true for the passage of time is perhaps not surprising, for the sociotemporal structure of social life is a general, almost inexorable, reality. That it is true for geographic areas of the city as well is a good deal more provocative, for Elyria is by no means a simple homogeneous aggregate. To the contrary, it is a collection of relatively diverse and distinct neighborhoods. Nonetheless, when it comes to police work, what is happening—and not when or where it happens—is the primary determinant of what the Elyria police will do in response.

Columbia, South Carolina. What are the empirical patterns behind police work in Columbia? Are there systematic variations in police action by day, time of day, type of action, or area of the city? More interestingly, are those variations similar in nature and magnitude to the variations uncovered in Elyria? With regard to the latter question, the comparisons we can build are limited; only one of the two measures of police action—police initiation of and police response time to logged events—that are available in Columbia is comparable to a counterpart indicator in Elyria. Granting that limitation, however, the answer to the comparative question is generally an affirmative one.

In Columbia, the gross level of police action is definitely not uniformly distributed across the days of the week or the hours of a typical day. With regard to the former, police calls occur disproportionately often on Fridays, Saturdays, and Sundays.[13] These three days account for 48.0 percent of the incidents handled by the Columbia police. By the same token, on any given day the hours from 10 A.M. to 3 P.M., 4 P.M. to 7 P.M., and 8 P.M. to 2 A.M. account for more than their 4.2 percent standard share of police events based on the random expectation, while the other hours account for less. The strongest hourly deviations from the standard come between 5 P.M. and 6 P.M., 9 P.M. and 11 P.M., and midnight and 1 A.M.[14] On the whole, gross levels of demand for police service in Columbia tend to peak during the evening and night hours of any given day and from Fridays through Sundays.

As was the case in Elyria, so is it the case in Columbia: the character of police action has a temporal dimension to it that is statistically significant but substantively modest. The overall rate of police proactivity in Columbia stands at 38.9 percent of the nonadministrative calls sampled from the police log, a rate nearly three times as large as that registered in Elyria. In Columbia, however, police proactivity rates tend to hit a trough on weekends, especially on Fridays and Saturdays, when neighborhood residents are most available for registering their own requests for local police service. Similarly, on any given day, police initiate a disproportionately high number of events between the hours of 2 A.M. and 7 A.M., and between 5 P.M. and 6 P.M. This hourly pattern is rather similar to that uncovered in Elyria, but the daily pattern in Columbia is somewhat at odds with its Elyria counterpart. In Columbia much more than in Elyria, police proactivity is more predictably a function of citizens' absence from or inattention to the neighborhood social scene. Even so, the magnitude of this function is small; the values of Cramer's V for the day-proactivity and hour-proactivity relationships in Columbia, .12 and .11 respectively, are not remarkable (as was also true in Elyria).

A similar pattern emerges when we focus on response times. Among all cases for which data are available (4725 to be precise), the Columbia police need an average of 3.29 minutes to respond to a "typical" event. Across days of the week, long-response days tend to be Thursdays, Fridays and Saturdays, when police are facing a growing proportion of citizen-initiated calls. Variations by hour take a similar rhythm; long-response hours are those between 7 A.M. and 10 A.M., noon and 1 P.M., 2 P.M. to 5 P.M., 6 P.M. to 7 P.M., 8 P.M. to 10 P.M., and midnight to 1 A.M. These are among the hours when police initiation rates are at their lowest. With regard to both of these variables, however, one-way analyses of variance generate relatively small F-ratios (2.14 for day, 2.58 for hour). In both cases, the effects of temporal variations on police response times are statistically significant, but substantively small.

A second source of potential variations in police action is the substantive nature of the incidents to which police attention is directed. As noted earlier, the Columbia police record their nonadministrative calls for service as falling into one of four broad types: serious (Part I) crimes, less serious (Part II) crimes and disputes, traffic-related events, and non-law-enforcement services. This is a relatively gross classification scheme, which precludes any analyses of specific types of calls or of the relevance of the property/nonproperty distinction to patterns of police action in Columbia. Hence, we can only turn directly to the effects of incident type on police proactivity rates and response times, which are summarized in table 4.7. Its structure is similar to that of table 4.5.

Staying strictly within the bounds of table 4.7, it is clear that the substantive classification of an event by police dispatchers and officers

Table 4.7. Event Types and Police Action in Columbia

Event Type:	Relative Frequency	Percent Police- Initiated	Mean Response Time (Minutes)
Serious Crime	6.5%	10.4%	4.57
Less Serious Crime, Disputes	38.5%	17.6%	4.36
Traffic Events	34.3%	75.2%	1.39
Service Events	20.7%	30.0%	3.30
	$\chi^2 = 1330.14$		$F = 59.0$
	$P = .001$		$P = .001$
	Cramer's $V = .54$		

in Columbia has a strong effect on how it will be handled by the police, and how quickly. The latter, of course, is due to the former; by definition, what the police initiate carries with it an instantaneous response time. Hence, it is no surprise that overall response rates for different types of calls are lowest for those where the likelihood of police initiation is highest, and vice versa. What is a bit more surprising is the power of type to partition the sources of initiation. In Columbia, traffic-related events are a good deal more than simply one among many alternative designations for instances of police work; from the proactivity rate listed for them in table 4.7, they would appear to constitute the substance of a veritable police offensive. This, in turn, suggests that police work in Columbia is probably a fair instance of the legalistic style. Traffic matters constitute roughly a third of the workload of the Columbia police, a sizable but not inordinate proportion. What traffic work they do, however, the Columbia police do proactively and aggressively—a benchmark of Wilson's distinction between legalistic and watchmanlike policing. In these data, type of event is strongly associated with police proactivity (Cramer's $V = .54$), and the substance of that association suggests a generally legalistic police department.

From a quick comparison of Elyria and Columbia with regard to the substantive content of local police action—specifically from a comparison of the first two columns of table 4.5 with those of table 4.7— both commonalities and differences emerge. In both cities, the bulk of the police workload is taken up with traffic matters and less serious crimes and disputes; in Columbia slightly more of the remaining effort

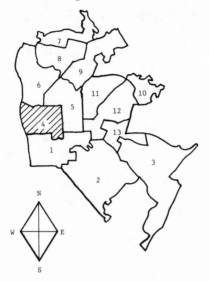

Note: Source Map -- 1970 Census.

Figure 4.3. Constructed Neighborhoods for Columbia, South Carolina

goes to services, while in Elyria slightly more goes to the handling of serious crimes. In both cities, the rank ordering of police proactivity by general incident types is the same; traffic is followed by services, disputes, and serious crimes. In each of these categories, however, the Columbia police are relatively more proactive than their Elyria counterparts, and substantially more so in traffic matters. Finally, in both cities types of events are more determinative of police initiation than is time of occurrence of the event; again, in Columbia this is even more strongly the case than in Elyria. While the data suggest that the Elyria and the Columbia police provide services to their respective cities in accordance with different styles, they also suggest that those differences are something closer to matters of degree than of kind.

Both time and type of event, and especially the latter, structure police action in Columbia. What, then, of ecology; do different areas of the city register different sorts of police events and evoke different sorts of responses? In Columbia, the problem of aligning police beats with census tracts to create neighborhood units of analysis has some of the same dimensions as in Elyria. At the time data were collected for this study, the Columbia police divided their city into 16 distinct

Table 4.8. Neighborhoods and Police Work in Columbia

Areas:	Relative Frequency	Percent Police-Initiated	Mean Response Time (Minutes)
1	18.8%	36.4%	2.96
2	13.3%	48.2%	1.88
3	7.4%	35.1%	4.65
4	12.4%	36.9%	3.25
5	5.1%	39.3%	3.64
6	7.9%	34.7%	3.48
7	4.0%	29.9%	5.16
8	7.2%	29.3%	5.43
9	5.7%	39.6%	2.65
10	4.1%	51.3%	2.95
11	6.3%	35.5%	2.89
12	3.8%	29.7%	4.29
13	4.0%	40.1%	3.37
	χ^2 =	56.71	F = 6.032
	P =	.001	P = .001
	Cramer's V =	.12	

patrol districts; in 1970, the U.S. Census Bureau included the city's population among all or part of 35 census tracts. To create the neighborhoods required for this analysis, the census tracts and patrol beats were aggregated in the same manner as described above for Elyria, until their boundaries came into near or perfect congruence. Figure 4.3 displays the territorial units of analysis created by this procedure. Area 4 in that figure contains the bulk of Columbia's downtown business district. Table 4.8 follows the map with a display of the relative distribution of calls across neighborhoods, the proactivity proportions, and the mean response times for calls in each neighborhood, as well as indicators of the significance of the effects of neighborhood differences on each of these variables.

In table 4.8 for neighborhoods, as in table 4.7 for substantive categories of events, there is a general correlation between police proactivity in a neighborhood and the speed of police response to its calls. Again, this is true by definition. When we focus on proactivity itself, we encounter a fairly wide range of variations across neighborhoods. Columbia's central business district, the bulk of which lies in area 4, is an area of only average relative police proactivity; variation on this measure would remain strong even were the downtown district excluded from the analysis. This, of course, is rather different from what was uncovered from the data for Elyria but, given the functional complexity of Columbia and the particular attraction that the institutions housed in various of its neighborhoods have for unattached young people, it is perhaps not so surprising.

In Columbia, as in Elyria, the area-action association is statistically significant but substantively weak; in fact, this relationship is of virtually identical magnitude across the two cities, with Cramer's V taking on a value of .12 in Columbia and .17 in Elyria. While Columbia is an even more diverse and complex urban entity than is Elyria, the neighborhood has relatively little effect on relative levels of police proactivity. In both cities, despite their demographic differences, what the police will do appears more a function of what is happening, rather than where or when.

Newark, New Jersey. Temporal variations also abound in the gross level of demand for police work in Newark. Calls are not distributed randomly across days of the week; rather, Saturdays in Newark are disproportionately demanding for the police, while Sundays and Wednesdays are relatively quiet.[15] Neither is the typical day a matter of random variations of calls across hours. Nine of the twelve hours between 1 P.M. and 1 A.M. register disproportionately high numbers of calls, with the honors in this regard going to the hours between 4 P.M. and 5 P.M., 7 P.M. and 10 P.M., and midnight to 1 A.M. From a patrol officer's perspective, things only really start to happen in Newark as the sun sets and the week rolls around to its end.

The dispatch log maintained by the Newark Police Department offers three measures of the character of police action: proactivity rates, event formalization rates, and average incident response times. All three have a statistically significant but substantively modest temporal dimension. In general terms, police proactivity in Newark is a function of the unavailability of most citizens to play roles as informal social control agents in their local neighborhoods. Proactivity is relatively high (that is, higher than the overall proportion of 34.0 percent logged events that are police-initiated) on Mondays, Wednesdays, and Thursdays, on weekdays, and during any given day between the hours of 3 A.M. and 4 A.M., 6 A.M. and 8 A.M., and 11 A.M. and 4 P.M. Average response times tend to follow these patterns as well, as they should; as we noted in the Columbia analysis, police-initiated events have virtually no response lapses, so days or hours of high proactivity should also be days or hours of low response times. While this is true in Newark as well, the pattern is not as strong or striking as it was in Columbia. On the average, Tuesdays, Thursdays, and Fridays tend to be long response days; weekend makes no difference; and, during the typical day, longer average responses tend to characterize the first half of the day (from 3 A.M. to 9 A.M. and from 10 A.M. to 2 P.M.). To some extent, then, there appears in Newark a tailoring of patrol work to effective citizen demand, with officers being more reactive when citizens are at home but attempting to respond more quickly to their demands for service. When most citizens are at work, Newark's police do slightly more proactive work and, as a result, need slightly more time to respond to the citizen demands that are registered. In all this, however, these differences are substantively unremarkable. Values of Cramer's V for daily and hourly variations in the police proactivity rate never exceed a modest .09; differences in mean response times across days or hours, while statistically significant, never exceed two minutes and are often a good deal smaller. While time may structure police patrol work in Newark, the degree to which it does so is—as it was in Elyria and Columbia—quite modest.

In Elyria, police proactivity and formalization of events by means of written reports were empirically linked (recall table 4.4); what the police initiated, they tended to formalize, and that tendency was a

Table 4.9. Event Formalization and Initiation in Newark

Source of Initiation:	Formalization	
	No	Yes
Police Officer	61.6%	38.4%
	(2353)	(1465)
Citizen	66.3%	33.7%
	(4916)	(2494)
Total	64.7%	35.3%
	(7269)	(3959)

$\chi^2 = 24.591$; d.f. = 1; $p = .001$.   Yule's $Q = -.10$

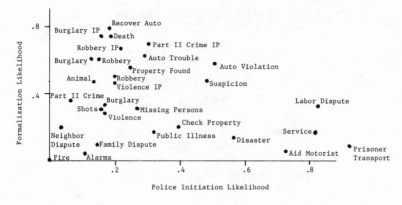

IP = In Progress

Note: Newark dispatchers use more than 150 event categories to record data.
The categories distinguish events by substantive type and immediacy
of occurrence. The categories used here were created by collapsing
the original categories across immediacy levels (with the exceptions
depicted in the figure) and by combining substantively similar events.

Figure 4.4. Event Analysis for Newark, New Jersey

strong and significant one (Yule's $Q = -.69$). In Newark, the same
empirical relationship emerges between proactivity and formalization,
but the magnitude of the link is not nearly so notable. Table 4.9
displays the relevant results. Formalization of events by the police in
Newark varies weakly by day, hour, and weekend, with higher rates of
formalization than the overall average of 35.3 percent tending to ac-
company periods of police proactivity and long response. These effects, however, are substantively quite modest. What is most notable
about formalization in Newark is the comparative anomaly uncovered
in its surprisingly small association with police proactivity vis-à-vis
that same relationship in Elyria.

What accounts for this comparative anomaly? Figure 4.4 provides
part of the answer with its distribution of different types of events in
Newark by both their police-initiation and formalization likelihoods.
This figure is roughly comparable to its counterpart for Elyria (figure
4.1) although the category labels for events differ somewhat across the
two cities. Granting this, note that in Newark as in Elyria formalized
events tend to differ from the nonformalized with regard to their
involvement with property. Note also, however, that Newark's police
tend not to formalize their dealings with prisoners quite so religiously
as do their counterparts in Elyria; neither are they as likely as the
Elyria police to initiate drunk driver incidents or auto violation events.

Table 4.10. Event Types and Police Action in Newark

Event Types:	Relative Frequency	Percent Police-Initiated	Percent Formal-ized	Mean Response Time (Minutes)
Serious Crime	30.2%	18.2%	56.4%	6.92
Less Serious Crime, Disputes	35.5%	25.3%	24.4%	5.94
Traffic Events	9.8%	32.4%	62.7%	5.90
Service Events	23.2%	56.7%	19.4%	2.55
	$\chi^2 = 1228.13$	$\chi^2 = 3439.8$		$F = 77.64$
	$P = $ .001	$P = $ .001		$P = $ .001
Cramer's $V = $	.30	$V = $ .33		

This, however, is only a proximate explanation; it simply pushes the question back a step, to inquire why these differences, in turn, might have emerged.

The answer to this latter query lies in what we might generally term the nature of "big-city policing" and is reflected most clearly in the four-way breakdown of general event types and their differential effects on the character of police action, as displayed in table 4.10. Unlike the case in Elyria or Columbia, the degree to which calls to handle serious crimes occupy the attention of the Newark police is strong, both absolutely and relatively. Such crime calls are most frequently citizen-initiated and most frequently formalized by reports; in fact, the police in Newark, and for that matter in any major American city, can often do little else in response to such calls other than file a report. Nonetheless, the larger portion of the police workload in Newark constituted by serious crimes is the key factor in forcing down the proactivity-formalization relationship. It in turn suggests that Newark occupies a relative middle-ground position with regard to a tentative general style designation for its distinctive brand of police work. By way of comparison, Newark's police are much less traffic-oriented than Columbia's and a good deal less proactive when they actually do traffic work; in short, the Newark police seem a good deal less legalistic than their Columbia counterparts. By the same token, however, they seem a good deal less watchmanlike than are officers in Elyria. They focus much more heavily on serious crimes and are uniformly more proactive for any type of event than are their Elyria counterparts. From these data, Newark seems to constitute a mix of types of police work that at least for the moment precludes any simple stylistic labeling.

Table 4.10 also underscores a finding uncovered in both Elyria and Columbia by essentially producing the same result for Newark: substantive type of call is far more critical to the structuring of police response than is time of occurrence of an event. This is true for all three of the dimensions of police action included in the table, and the strength of the relationship is of an order of magnitude similar to that uncovered for comparable indicators in the other two cities. On police proactivity, the only indicator comparable across all three cities, the Newark police are more proactive than their Elyria counterparts on all types of calls, and more proactive than Columbia's on all but traffic calls. Because Columbia appears to be such a special case in this latter regard, the strength of the proactivity-type relationship in Newark is more similar to that in Elyria than to that in Columbia. Nonetheless, in all three cities, it is the type of call that structures police action much more notably than the time of its occurrence.

In both Elyria and Columbia, police action had a territorial context;

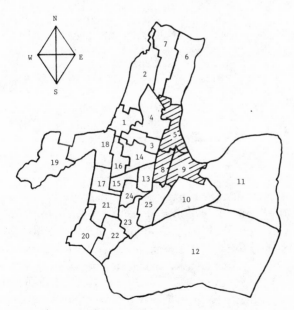

Figure 4.5. Constructed Neighborhoods for Newark, New Jersey

Table 4.11. Neighborhoods and Police Action in Newark

Areas:	Relative Frequency	Percent Police-Initiated	Percent Formal-ized	Mean Response Time (Minutes)
1	5.1%	39.6%	33.2%	4.38
2	3.7%	22.8%	36.9%	6.26
3	3.5%	28.9%	31.0%	4.77
4	4.2%	26.6%	37.0%	5.38
5	7.8%	39.2%	40.9%	5.07
6	4.8%	28.3%	38.5%	5.61
7	3.6%	28.5%	36.9%	5.90
8	4.4%	38.0%	40.5%	5.14
9	7.4%	40.1%	33.8%	5.20
10	3.5%	25.5%	40.4%	5.92
11	4.3%	39.9%	34.8%	4.90
12	4.8%	29.9%	28.9%	7.19
13	4.0%	33.1%	28.5%	5.29
14	2.4%	35.8%	35.3%	5.45
15	2.4%	18.9%	25.2%	6.65
16	2.8%	24.5%	32.6%	5.88
17	3.2%	22.1%	38.5%	8.06
18	4.1%	23.8%	31.2%	6.96
19	4.2%	27.0%	43.2%	6.58
20	4.6%	20.6%	44.1%	7.06
21	4.0%	22.8%	39.4%	6.83
22	3.2%	25.5%	44.9%	7.02
23	3.0%	29.5%	37.0%	6.75
24	2.0%	21.3%	36.8%	7.41
25	2.7%	33.7%	31.3%	7.34
	$\chi^2 = 220.24$		$\chi^2 = 726.95$	$F = 4.82$
	$P = .001$		$P = .001$	$P = .001$
	Cramer's $V = .15$		$V = .11$	

in both, however, neither territory nor time could match substantive type as a determinant of police proactivity, event formalization, or average response time. Figure 4.5 depicts the 25 neighborhood areas on which the territorial analysis for Newark is based. These areas were created by aggregating census tracts and patrol beats—there were initially 96 of the former and 28 of the latter—until their boundaries came into contiguity or near-contiguity, the same process used to define corresponding areas in Elyria and Columbia. Figure 4.5 also highlights the three areas in Newark partly or completely composed of the city's downtown business district. Table 4.11 displays frequency distributions of calls across these areas, values of the available indicators of police action in each, indicators of the magnitude of the area-action relationships and results for the associated significance tests.

The central business district areas of Newark (Areas 5, 8, and 9) in figure 4.5 are indeed somewhat more likely to be the scenes of more proactive police work and, as a result, of lower police response times than are the other neighborhoods of the city, and they tend (albeit weakly) to fall at the high end of the continuum on formalization likelihood as well. The tendency in this regard is weak, however; in fact, that seems to be the message of table 4.11 in general. Areas vary with regard to the kind of police work they experience, but the variations in this regard are not very powerful. Area-action relationships in Newark are statistically significant but substantively weak. In this, they neatly replicate what was also true in Elyria and Columbia; across these three cities, neighborhood and relative police proactivity are linked to degrees of only Cramer's V equal to .17 in Elyria, .12 in Columbia, and .15 in Newark. For all the internal neighborhood variations that characterize each, and for all the social, economic, and demographic differences that separate each from the other, this consistency seems rather remarkable.

Conclusion

Anyone who has ridden or walked with police officers or detectives on patrol has sensed the changing tenor of the job across shifts, as the busy, exciting, and sometimes demanding hours of the evening turn into the dull and boring hours of the early morning. Similarly, a relatively short walk or ride can usually transport that same observer from tranquil neighborhoods where police presence is appreciated and highly regarded to others of the less tranquil variety where police are seen as—and often actually are—little more than an invading army of outsiders.[16] Further, anyone who has accompanied police in two or more different jurisdictions will note that police work has a palpably different "feel" from one city to another. All of these variations are captured and recorded by the data typically available in a police dispatch log, as is evidenced by the empirical analyses of such data reported in this chapter.

George Kelling's statement that "the dispatch system determines the context within with the patrol officer works" receives direct confirmation from the results reported here. In all three cities studied, it is the substantive label attached to an event—a label that police develop internally and for their own purposes of resource allocation and service provision—that goes farthest to pattern the character of the work police officers do in response to that event. Time and territory pattern police action as well, but not nearly to the same degree.

Because substantive type of event and police proactivity are as closely linked as they are in Elyria, Columbia, and Newark research that deals with both simultaneously—in a combined measure that systematically and reliably captures the major sources of variations in local police work——is virtually demanded. Such a measure would appear to constitute the very heart of the idea of a police style by combining a sense of what the police do with how they do it. Toward the development of that measure and the uncovering of its determinants we now turn.

Notes

1. One of the pioneers in developing this method for the scientific study of work, and one who has applied the time budget in a variety of research situations, has been Henry Mintzberg. See Mintzberg (1973) for a general description of time-budget data collection procedures.

2. In the more sophisticated dispatch systems, a record is made of the unit that responded to each logged event. Thus, it is theoretically possible to collect data on the police incidents handled by individual units which, in turn, makes theoretically possible the kinds of analyses and inferences from action to attitude suggested above. Note, however, that such a procedure would mean in practical terms gathering data on virtually everything handled by a police department over an extended time period, in order to produce a reliable set of data on individuals' working patterns. For all but the most massive of studies, that is a practical impossibility.

3. There is empirical evidence to suggest that they need not do so (Kansas City Police Department 1977), but most American police agencies operate in this vein nonetheless.

4. Even where logs can be manipulated, those manipulations are such as to reflect an important reality of the field situation. Two such possibilities for manipulation are generally the most common. On the one hand, citizens can inflate the importance of the events they report, in order to assure that police will put a relatively high priority on responding to their calls. Even when citizens do this, however, the police have little way of knowing it in

advance of an actual encounter; they must and do respond to the call as reported. On the other hand, police can inflate the length of time it takes them to service a given reported incident. When they do this, they usually do it in order to catch up on a report, to allow for a few seconds of further investigation, or simply to catch their breaths and settle their nerves after a particularly trying experience. These inflations, however, amount to little more than a few seconds or minutes; neither dispatchers nor patrol supervisors will allow for anything more without checking on the unit involved. In neither event do these manipulations of the dispatch log falsify the reality of the police response to an incident. To the contrary, both are valid reflections of how the job is, and probably must be, performed in the field.

5. The specific days were as follows:

Thursday, January 17	Sunday, July 13
Tuesday, February 19	Monday, July 28
Wednesday, March 12	Wednesday, September 24
Tuesday, March 25	Thursday, October 23
Wednesday, April 23	Friday, October 24
Monday, April 28	Friday, October 31
Thursday, May 8	Tuesday, November 11
Wednesday, May 21	Friday, November 14
Monday, June 2	Saturday, November 15
Saturday, June 28	Sunday, November 23

6. Amounting, according to those reports, to approximately 10%.
7. It is worth recalling, however, that the time of day captured in these data is the time at which a police department was informed of an event. Often, that is nearly the same as the time at which the event actually happened, but often—as in the case where a burglary is discovered after some absence from a home or business—it is not. Since our concern here is the nature of police work, our measure is appropriate. Nonetheless, we should be clear on the point that it measures the genesis of police awareness of an event, and not necessarily that of the event itself.
8. As noted in the discussions of data availability and quality, the dispatch logs in all three of our subject police agencies contain incidents of a purely administrative nature. These involve no contacts with citizens, and result in no police services of any type being provided. They are, in short, the organizational maintenance tasks without the completion of which a police agency cannot operate, but with which we are not particularly concerned. In the descriptions and analyses reported from here on, such cases are excluded from consideration.
9. Most social researchers pay little attention to time in their studies, at least in the sense of daily or hourly time. A few, however, have made it the centerpiece of some very revealing analytical and empirical work. The most outstanding of them is undoubtedly Zerubavel (1981).

10. Frequency distributions for the sampled calls by day of the week, by weekend and by hour of the day are as follows:

Day of the Week

Monday	12.5% (312 events)	Friday	15.4% (383 events)
Tuesday	14.2% (353 events)	Saturday	17.1% (426 events)
Wednesday	13.3% (332 events)	Sunday	13.1% (326 events)
Thursday	14.4% (360 events)		

Weekend

No	62.5% (1551 events)	Yes	37.5% (929 events)

Hour of the Day

12–1 A.M. 5.2% (130)	12–1 P.M. 4.2% (104)
1–2 A.M. 4.3% (106)	1–2 P.M. 4.8% (118)
2–3 A.M. 4.0% (100)	2–3 P.M. 4.2% (105)
3–4 A.M. 3.4% (85)	3–4 P.M. 4.2% (105)
4–5 A.M. 1.5% (38)	4–5 P.M. 4.8% (120)
5–6 A.M. 1.7% (42)	5–6 P.M. 4.3% (107)
6–7 A.M. 1.9% (47)	6–7 P.M. 4.0% (98)
7–8 A.M. 3.0% (75)	7–8 P.M. 4.2% (105)
8–9 A.M. 4.6% (115)	8–9 P.M. 4.7% (116)
9–10 A.M. 4.0% (99)	9–10 P.M. 5.2% (129)
10–11 A.M. 4.1% (102)	10–11 P.M. 5.7% (141)
11–Noon 5.0% (124)	11–12 6.8% (169)

11. Because the data from each study site in this research constitute a sample of the universe of police events, it is appropriate to conduct tests of statistical significance for the distributions in contingency tables based on them and to report those test results. Note, however, that most of these data are nominal or ordinal measures, and recall that the base of sampled cases in each city is quite large. Because of the former, we would normally have recourse to the Chi-squared test statistic; because of the latter, however, that statistic will uncover "significant" results for all but the most trivial variations about the general frequency distributions. In reporting results, then, we will certainly note the failure of a joint distribution to attain statistical significance as a result of this test but, even where it succeeds in that, we will base substantive conclusions more on the magnitude and direction of an appropriate measure of association (like Yule's Q in table 4.4) than on the results of the significance test.

12. That is undesirable for research purposes, but understandable from a practical standpoint. Recall that the dispatch log in Elyria is maintained manually. Such recoding would be a mammoth task and one of dubious utility when subsequent research using this material would require further hand tabulation.

13. The simple frequency distribution is as follows:

Monday	1073 events (14.9%)	Friday	1129 events (15.7%)
Tuesday	1055 events (14.7%)	Saturday	1170 events (16.3%)
Wednesday	813 events (11.3%)	Sunday	1152 events (16.0%)
Thursday	788 events (11.0%)		

14. The simple frequency distribution is as follows:

12–1 A.M. 369 calls (5.2%)	12–1 P.M. 350 calls (4.9%)
1–2 A.M. 331 calls (4.7%)	1–2 P.M. 312 calls (4.4%)
2–3 A.M. 264 calls (3.7%)	2–2 P.M. 364 calls (5.1%)
3–4 A.M. 227 calls (3.2%)	3–4 P.M. 238 calls (3.3%)
4–5 A.M. 183 calls (2.6%)	4–5 P.M. 343 calls (4.8%)
5–6 A.M. 113 calls (1.6%)	5–6 P.M. 382 calls (5.4%)
6–7 A.M. 124 calls (1.7%)	6–7 P.M. 322 calls (4.5%)
7–8 A.M. 160 calls (2.2%)	7–8 P.M. 280 calls (3.9%)
8–9 A.M. 259 calls (3.6%)	8–9 P.M. 322 calls (4.5%)
9–10 A.M. 260 calls (3.7%)	9–10 P.M. 415 calls (5.8%)
10–11 A.M. 362 calls (5.1%)	10–11 P.M. 429 calls (6.0%)
11–Noon 347 calls (4.9%)	11–12 P.M. 362 calls (5.1%)

15. The simple frequency distribution in this regard is as follows:

Monday	1661 events (14.5%)	Friday	1659 events (14.4%)
Tuesday	1604 events (14.0%)	Saturday	2004 events (17.4%)
Wednesday	1466 events (12.8%)	Sunday	1457 events (12.7%)
Thursday	1636 events (14.2%)		

16. Those who have not conducted such observations at first hand can nonetheless experience them, vividly if vicariously, in the pages of Skolnick (1967), Rubinstein (1973) or Muir (1977).

5. The Elements of Police Style

What is a police style? How do we know it when we see it and, based on that recognition, how do we capture it for research purposes? Further, on what basis should it be so captured; where, in any given empirical situation, should we hope to see police styles enacted? To this point, we have generally skirted the task of offering a full, formal answer to any of these questions, but that task can be skirted no longer.

The conceptualization of police style offered below, and the measurements based on that, follow from the general outlines offered in chapter 4. We have noted that a police style is at least (1) a behavioral pattern that (2) is total or nearly so, and (3) that is characteristic among aggregates of police officers. The first of these dimensions suggests that police style is not equivalent to police visibility or relative strength, although visibility and strength may well be necessary but not sufficient causes for the emergence of a given style. The second dimension suggests that police styles are not equivalent to the levels of arrests that are made in police jurisdictions (surely instances of legalistic policing but comprising relatively little of that totality of actions constituting local police work.) Finally, the third dimension suggests that a police style is not a matter of a free choice to be made by a police officer acting on his or her own but rather a common pattern of action enacted by groups of officers based on their shared understandings of the work to be performed, the organization housing them, and the environments in which they are to function.

The first two of these three dimensions require, in a nutshell, that we collect and analyze more and different data than are typically available for a secondary analysis of police action; the data accessible from a police dispatch log seem quite well suited for that. The third dimension is a bit more complex in what it requires, as it raises the issue of aggregation of data without specifying the appropriate unit of analysis to which those data should be cumulated. As noted in the preceding chapter, that issue is resolved here on a territorial basis, in favor of the local subcommunity or neighborhood that experiences a variety of police work. An extended word about that choice is in order.

The Locus of Styles: Two Conflicting Arguments

James Q. Wilson originally constructed his typology of police styles at the organizational level of analysis. Each style was analyzed as the collective organizational response of a police agency to differing community socioeconomic characteristics and political structures, and to different local conceptions of social order. Wilson did not, however, systematically consider the possibility that differing demands might be placed on an individual police officer by various of those with whom the officer comes into contact. Nevertheless, in all but the smallest police agencies serving the most homogeneous communities, this possibility seems intuitively plausible, especially among those police—like patrol officers—whose roles dictate that they deal with the general public in a relatively diffuse context. Such officers function to uphold "law and order," but they usually enter the community with relatively vague notions from their formal training of the concrete referents of that phrase (Harris 1973; Van Maanen 1975). In their early street assignments, they face differing and often conflicting expectations about their activities emanating from the communities they patrol (Black 1970; Black and Reiss 1970), the more experienced officers with whom they work (Van Maanen 1975), and both the city executives and the police administrators who set the overall policies for the police department (Bordua and Reiss 1966). In short, when the demands of the clientele, the occupational culture, and the organizational hierarchy are not at least parallel to each other, they can pose a noteworthy role conflict for the police officer, unless of course, the demands coming from any one of these so clearly outweigh the others to virtually force an unambiguous response.

To define style as an organizational characteristic of the police is to assume that conflicts about styles faced by individual officers are generally resolved in favor of the demands of the police hierarchy. The literature on the discretion of rank-and-file members of public-sector service agencies throws some doubt on this assumption. The discretion of "street-level bureaucrats" in human service agencies seems only imperfectly controllable by organizational managers (Blau 1963; Prottas 1978; Lipsky 1980), and this is equally true among police (Tifft 1975; Rubinstein 1973; Muir 1977). In turn, this fact implies that police style will vary within as well as across police departments. It also implies that style is essentially a response negotiated by individual officers, or perhaps by small groups of police, to the various demands placed on them, and therefore a response that will vary notably across different groups or categories of officers.

This seemingly plausible argument can be countered almost equally well by one that focuses on the police organization as the predominant source of style demands placed on individual police. This is, of course, the argument that underlies Wilson's work. It posits not so much the absence of conflicting style demands as their general resolution in favor of organizational dictates; in empirical terms, it leads us to expect style heterogeneity across police agencies and homogeneity within them. Support for this argument comes from a consideration of the organizational realities of policing in the United States. Consider, first, that career mobility across American police departments is exceedingly infrequent. Except at the very highest and lowest ranks, lateral entry is simply not a typical option for the officer seeking advancement. Promotion to higher ranks is almost invariably made from within a department and that, coupled frequently with nonportable pensions and terms of accrued seniority, puts a premium on remaining in place. Effectively, then, the organization is the career; an officer is overwhelmingly likely to enter and retire from the same agency. Now add to this the second relevant fact: that the trend toward professionalization so widely heralded in American policing for the past twenty years (Caiden 1977) has, for all practical purposes, been one of increasing centralization. We can readily grant that the trend may have taken hold to different degrees in differing departments, varying with the ways in which local police executives are held accountable to urban political officials (Bordua and Reiss 1966). The fact remains that it *has* been a general trend and that it has attempted to increase the degree of control of police executives over their subordinates. Once police executives determine on a given style, "professional" centralization better enables them to see that it is carried out by officers with strong incentives to do so if they do not want to jeopardize their careers.

All this suggests, using Albert Hirschman's terms (1970), that police officers are more likely to remain loyal to their superiors than to voice their objections publicly or resign in protest. Thus, patterns of police action will be homogeneous within but heterogeneous across a set of police departments.

One of the major purposes of this book is to put competing arguments like these to an empirical test. The need for comparisons that range simultaneously across cities and across the internal components of cities makes the local neighborhood or community area an appropriate unit of analysis for achieving such ends.

The Dimensions of Style: Issues in Measurement

As we noted earlier, there is relatively little guidance forthcoming from the literature on the best means for capturing police styles in one or more empirical measures, primarily because relatively few studies have addressed the issue. Thus, the best place to start searching for such measures is probably with Wilson's original treatment:

> In some communities, the police in dealing with situations that do not involve "serious" crime act as if *order maintenance* rather than law enforcement were their principal function. . . . To the extent the administrator can influence the discretion of his men, he does so by allowing them to ignore many common minor violations . . . to use the law more as a means of maintaining order than of regulating conduct. . . . The police are watchman-like not simply in emphasizing order over law enforcement but also in judging the seriousness of infractions less by what the law says about them than by their immediate and personal consequences, which will differ in importance depending on the standards of the relevant group—teenagers, Negroes, prostitutes, motorists, families and so forth. . . . The police style in these cities is watchmanlike because, with certain exceptions dictated by the chief's policies or the city's expectations, the patrolman is allowed—even encouraged—to follow the path of least resistance in carrying out his daily, routine assignments. . . . The police handle the problem of an adversary relationship with the public by withdrawing from as many such relationships as possible. (Wilson 1972: 140–144)
>
> In some departments, the officer is expected to take a *law enforcement* view of his role . . . to handle commonplace situations as if they were matters of law

enforcement rather than order maintenance. . . . A legalistic department will issue traffic tickets at a high rate, detain and arrest a high proportion of juvenile offenders, act vigorously against illicit enterprises, and make a large number of misdemeanor arrests even when, as with petty larceny, the public order has not been breached. . . . The police will act, on the whole, as if there were a single standard of community conduct—that which the law prescribes. (ibid., pp. 172–174).

In some communities, the police take seriously all requests for either law enforcement or order maintenance . . . but are less likely to respond by making an arrest or imposing formal sanctions. . . . The police intervene frequently but not formally . . . the police can act as if their task were to estimate the "market" for police services and to produce a "product" that meets the demand. . . . Such a policy will be called the *"service"* style. Serious matters—burglaries, robberies, assaults—are of course taken seriously and thus "suspicious" persons are carefully watched or questioned. But with regard to minor infractions of the law, arrests are avoided when possible . . . but there will be frequent use of informal, nonarrest sanctions. (ibid., pp. 200–201)

Both in these particular quotations and in the general narrative from which they are drawn, Wilson seems to focus on two crosscutting variables as being more or less determinative of a police department's style. The first of these is the level of police officers' aggressiveness in searching out instances for the application of their craft, the degree to which they are proactive. While it is not clear where a service-oriented agency fits in this distinction, it is fairly certain that Wilson sees an equation between proactive and legalist departments on the one hand, and reactive and watchmanlike agencies on the other. In the former, officers are expected to be active enforcers of an impartial law; in the latter, their role is more one of "keeping the lid on." The proactive/reactive dichotomy seems to capture this facet of style rather well.

Wilson also pays some attention to the substantive types of calls handled by police in his study sites, as well as to the sources of initiation of those calls. In this regard, he seems to distinguish non-law-enforcement services from traffic-related events and these, in turn, from crimes, disputes and disorders. From his account, service calls clearly seem the prerogative of the service-oriented agency, regardless of who—a citizen or an officer—initiates the call for police assistance. The power of the other two to distinguish types of departments depends on the frequency of their occurrence and the source of their initiation. Agencies in which officers on their own initiative make many arrests, give traffic citations, and intervene in local disputes are those Wilson would term legalistic; where officers are more reactive in all of these matters and are less intrusive in the flow of local social life, Wilson would probably term their departments more watchmanlike.

These two aspects of police work can and probably should be treated as separate dimensions of police style for, depending on how they are measured, they need not necessarily be highly correlated. Aggressiveness implies an incidence-based measure derived, to be true to Wilson's definition, from all instances of police-initiated activity and, perhaps, from all nontraffic police-initiated events.[1] Type or style, as discussed here as a combination of the substantive nature of an event and the source of its initiation, implies a proportional measure, indicating the relative mix of different styles in a department's workload as a whole or that part of it attributable to any of the given neighborhoods that it polices. The two may be empirically related, but then again they need not be. In any particular city or neighborhood, the mix of calls handled by police could be heavily weighted toward the watchmanlike—few police-initiated events and few non-law-enforcement services offered—and yet the police could still be relatively aggressive, were that city or neighborhood a small one. The degree to which aggressiveness and substantive style are related in any given setting is thus an empirical question.

From the materials available from the police dispatch logs in Elyria, Columbia, and Newark can be drawn the specific elements necessary for measuring and analyzing both police aggressiveness and substantive police style. In light of what was just said, we will present separate analyses for each of these dimensions of police action, pulling them together in a concluding treatment that addresses a series of hypotheses about their city-level determinants.

Aggressiveness

It seems rather obvious that police aggressiveness as a concept and police initiation of action as a measure are closely linked; police-initiated events are little more than the raw materials from which a measure of aggressiveness can be built. The only real question to be resolved about their linkage is the basis on which police-initiated events are to be counted: as a proportion of all calls received and handled, or as a rate per unit of population served. Wilson's original treatment of the types of police style argues for rate per unit, and his subsequent research (Wilson and Boland 1978) pursues that argument with some interesting results, so that lead is generally followed here. Nonetheless, the treatment that follows presents results based on proportion of calls as well, for the caveat about the lack of a necessary relationship between aggressiveness as an incidence measure and proportion of calls constituting a particular style designation applies here equally well.

Table 5.1 displays the incidence rates and the relative proportions of police-initiated events for Elyria, Columbia, and Newark. Two sets of figures are presented for each city, one based on all nonadministrative incidents handled by police departments and one based on all nonadministrative and nontraffic incidents. This distinction is offered in the attempt to control for possible fluctuations in the overall rates and proportions based on a temporary traffic initiative in any given department that might mask the style of its work-product in other, more ordinary circumstances.

Table 5.1. Police Aggressiveness in Elyria, Columbia and Newark (Citywide Totals)

| | Police-Initiated Events | |
	Annual Inci-dence Rate (Per 1000 Population)	Relative Proportion
Elyria, Ohio		
All Non-Administrative Events	58.04	13.4
All Non-Administrative, Non-Traffic Events	20.87	7.3
Columbia, South Carolina		
All Non-Administrative Events	323.56	38.9
All Non-Administrative, Non-Traffic Events	114.97	20.8
Newark, New Jersey		
All-Non Administrative Events	204.35	34.0
All Non-Administrative, Non-Traffic Events	174.09	31.4

As is clear from table 5.1, the decision to exclude traffic events is critical for both measures of police aggressiveness presented. Without such events, incidence rates and relative proportions fall in all three cities, albeit more so in Elyria and especially in Columbia than in Newark. Given the relative importance of traffic calls in the workloads of Elyria and Columbia, which was noted in the preceding chapter, this is not all that surprising. Further, and more importantly, the exclusion of traffic calls changes the relative ordering of the three police agencies; Newark emerges from the more controlled comparison as the most aggressive police department, Elyria as the least, and Columbia in a middle ground position slightly closer to Newark.

The pattern of findings displayed in table 5.1 is consistent with the variations of the three police departments with regard to their absolute and their relative levels of strength. These variables take on respective values of 76 and 1.303 in Elyria,[2] 276 and 2.727 in Columbia, and 1189 and 3.611 in Newark. Table 5.1 now offers at least circumstantial evidence to support the inference that the larger the police department and/or the more visible its personnel relative to the city population, the more aggressively will patrol officers conduct themselves in the field. This pattern of association holds most clearly for the "pure" figures measuring aggressiveness—those based on nonadministrative *and* nontraffic cases from the dispatch logs. The relationship is a bit more tenuous when the more unrefined set of measures are used for the comparison.

Lest too much be invested in this apparent relationship between aggressiveness and size, it is necessary that these indicators of police aggressiveness be disaggregated to the neighborhood level of analysis. Measures calculated on a citywide basis run the risk of being skewed by outlying cases that are particularly different from the more normal variety. Further, they run the risk of being completely misleading if they come from bimodal or otherwise "odd" underlying distributions. In the context of police work, the first possibility would arise where a specific type of neighborhood—say, for the sake of illustration, one containing a public housing project—received more aggressive police work than did any other. Citywide measures of aggressiveness would be skewed upward as a result. The second would arise where officers followed a regional strategy of policing tailored to neighborhood variations and demands which differed markedly from one part of town to another. This latter might well be the outcome expected with territorial decentralization of a department into district stations, or with the conduct of locality-based experimental programs like team policing. In such situations, citywide measures of aggressiveness might well take on mid-range, substantively meaningless values.

Table 5.2 and Figure 5.1 present the findings on police aggressiveness based on this neighborhood focus. Again, the table presents both incidence rates and relative proportions for all three cities of interest here. In this instance, citywide totals represent average values calculated across the constituent neighborhoods in each city studied; that is, the figures presented in table 5.2 represent averages calculated across the relevant neighborhood incidence rates and proportions. Figure 5.1 displays the positions of individual neighborhoods in each of the cities on both their aggressiveness rates and proactivity proportions. All of these data elements, further, are based on nonadministrative, nontraffic calls to exclude possible effects caused by temporary traffic enforcement initiatives. The neighborhoods on which these rates and proportions are calculated are those that were depicted in chapter 4.

There are a number of points worth noting from these figures. First, as table 5.2 demonstrates, the rank ordering of Elyria, Columbia, and

Table 5.2. Police Aggressiveness at the Neighborhood Level

	Police-Initiated Events	
	Incidence Rate	Proportion of Area Total
Elyria, Ohio		
All Neighborhood Areas ($N = 12$)	30.5	6.6
All Residential Neighborhood Areas ($N = 11$)	18.8	5.6
Columbia, South Carolina		
All Neighborhood Areas ($N = 13$)	91.5	13.4
All Residential Neighborhood Areas ($N = 12$)	81.2	13.3
Newark, New Jersey		
All Neighborhood Areas ($N = 25$)	156.4	27.4
All Residential Neighborhood Areas ($N = 22$)	104.4	26.0

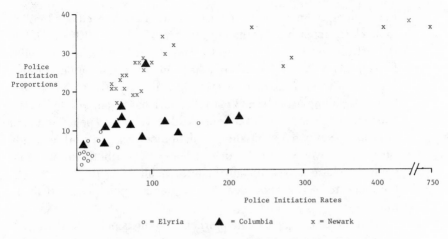

Figure 5.1. Police Aggressiveness in the Neighborhoods

Newark on nontraffic or "pure" police aggressiveness remains the same as it was before, despite the different method of rate and proportion calculation. Newark still experiences the most aggressive police work and Elyria the least; Columbia still occupies a middle ground— more like Newark from the standpoint of incidence rates of police aggressiveness, and more like Elyria from the perspective of the proportional measures. As the former is the measure truest to Wilson's original emphasis and his subsequent research as well, it seems clear from a comparison of tables 5.1 and 5.2 that the simple city-level measures and the aggregated neighborhood-level measures are indeed tapping the same general reality.

Method of calculation of the measure of police aggressiveness does make a difference, even if not a startling one. That is the second point to emerge from table 5.2 and a comparison of it with the relevant figures in table 5.1. That difference is consistent across the three cities studied here; in each, the rate of overall police aggressiveness is lower when those rates are aggregated across neighborhoods than when they are calculated as citywide totals. In each city, then, there is indeed some skew in the data. That is, in each a handful of neighborhoods experience police work that is markedly more aggressive than is the case in other parts of the same city. The distributions in figure 5.1 demonstrate that rather vividly, and thus help to pinpoint the problem cases. In general, there is a rough clustering of neighborhoods in the figure along the incidence dimension, with areas in each city tending to lie closer to each other than to those in other cities. Elyria exhibits this pattern to a striking degree, Columbia and Newark less markedly. In each case, however, there are a handful of extreme outliers. Elyria has one, with an incidence rate at approximately 160; Columbia has two, both falling near the 200 mark; Newark has three, with two in the 400–450 range and one at the remarkable level of 750 police-initiated nontraffic events per thousand population per year. In all three study sites, police work in these "deviant" areas contributes to a simple citywide total that is artificially high for, in all three, the other neighborhoods receive a good deal less aggressive police work than do these.

What are these special neighborhoods? Why is police work in each so aggressive? A simple explanation that accounts for the status of five of the six—the one in Elyria, one of the two in Columbia, and all three in Newark—comes by noting one simple fact: all five are composed predominantly, if not completely, of the central business district in their respective cities.[3] In all these areas, the size of the resident population is small and land use is predominantly institutional or commercial. Central business districts in these cities—in most American cities for that matter—are relatively anomic places, designed more for the use and convenience of transients and commuters than for residents. As Black (1976) has argued, where means of informal social control are ineffective or nonexistent, resort will and must be had to more formal vehicles and means. In central business districts, what few residents there are have few means at their disposal to exercise informal social control over local events. Both they and the police know this; the data suggest that the police attempt aggressively to fill the resulting social control "gaps."

Taken together, these findings suggest that two primary variables work to generate police aggressiveness: size of the police agency (which was noted in chapter 2 to be a primary function of city size and degree of urbanization) and status of the locality experiencing that aggressiveness as a central business district. In short, the evidence suggests that larger departments police their cities more aggressively than smaller ones, and that any department polices its city's central business district more aggressively than it does the residential neighborhoods. Granting this latter condition, however, there appears to be relatively little to distinguish policing in one neighborhood from that in another, despite the internal variations in each city studied.

Substantive Effort

The methodological problems inherent in trying to create a content-based measure of police style are a bit more complicated than those involved in measuring aggressiveness. In building the former, we must recognize: (1) that the categories of Wilson's original typology are not themselves empirical entities; to the contrary, every police department will constitute a mix of the three types of style in varying proportions; (2) that neighborhoods within a city may vary with regard to the predominant style of police work they experience but that, again, no neighborhood will receive only one style of policing; and, of course (3) that cities will probably vary with regard to style, even granting that each will mix some of each discrete style into its total experience of police work. We need, in short, to apply Wilson's typology in this study to individual calls for police service and then to count and compare calls of a given type across our study sites and within and among their constituent neighborhoods.

For this research, the application of the typology to the sampled dispatch cases followed a set of coding rules that closely conforms to Wilson's logic in constructing the original typology. Table 5.3 effectively summarizes those coding rules. Non-law-enforcement services were designated as service-oriented calls, regardless of their origin; all other events were labeled legalistic if they were officer-initiated and watchmanlike if they were citizen-initiated.[4] The application of this particular set of coding rules to the available data necessarily deals with broad rather than narrow substantive categories of cases because the data are subject to something of a "least common denominator"

Table 5.3. Coding Rules for Classifying Police Events

	Source of Initiation	
Original Call Type	*Officer*	*Citizen*
Traffic	LEGALIST	WATCHMAN
Crime/Disorder	LEGALIST	WATCHMAN
Service	SERVICE	SERVICE

type of problem. Recall that the dispatch logs from Elyria and Newark contained rich detail on types of incidents, but the Columbia dispatch system used only the broad designations of serious crime, less serious crime and disorder, traffic, and service to distinguish the events its officers handle. While the Elyria and Newark information can be recoded to be consistent with the designations applied in Columbia in order to achieve comparability across cities, it is nonetheless true that such a broad coding scheme may not be the optimal tool with which to study style. By way of example, note that a family fight resolved by an officer without recourse to formal legal action is substantively both a service provided and a disorder resolved. The coding scheme used here emphasizes the latter aspect of such a situation, and not the former; for such incidents, it undercounts the degree to which an agency is "service-oriented." It would obviously be preferable to know a good deal more about the dynamics of the event and the motivations of the officer(s) handling it before applying a style label to it, but such data are not available here. The best we can do is count consistently across agencies, in a manner that at the least has plausibility as an operational version of the Wilson schema.

Table 5.4 presents the results of the application of these coding rules to the Elyria, Columbia, and Newark dispatch data. The first panel of the table presents simple frequency distributions of types of call for each city. The second compares styles across each pair of cities by means of the index of dissimilarity. In essence, this measure reports the proportion of calls in any one city that would have to be redistributed across the style categories to achieve an overall distribu-

Table 5.4. Police Calls Distributed by Style Categories

	Service	Watchman	Legalist
Elyria, Ohio	16.7	69.4	13.8
Columbia, South Carolina	20.7	37.4	41.9
Newark, New Jersey	23.2	53.7	23.4

INDICES OF DISSIMILARITY

	Elyria	Columbia	Newark
Elyria	—	.325	.159
Columbia	—	—	.187
Newark	—	—	—

Table 5.5. Traffic Calls and Style Categorizations

City	Traffic Tickets/ Traffic Calls per 1000 Population	Style Category
Albany, New York	11.4	Watchman
Amsterdam, New York	16.4	Watchman
NEWARK, NEW JERSEY	30.3	WATCHMAN
ELYRIA, OHIO	37.2	WATCHMAN
Newburgh, New York	40.9	Watchman
Brighton, New York	61.0	Service
Nassau County, New York	61.0	Service
Highland Park, Illinois	97.8	Legalist
Syracuse, New York	109.1	Legalist
COLUMBIA, SOUTH CAROLINA	208.6	LEGALIST
Oakland, California	247.7	Legalist

(For data and classifications on the Wilson case studies, see Wilson, 1972:95, 141, 172, 200)

tion identical to that in the city against which it is paired. Following this, table 5.5 attempts to locate Elyria, Columbia, and Newark in the police style typology originally offered by Wilson for his eight case study sites. Table 5.5 reproduces his original values on the traffic ticket index calculated for each of his eight study sites, and the resulting style categories to which he allocated each. Our three cities, are included among these cases on the basis of their respective police-initiated traffic incidence rates. This measure is not perfectly comparable with that used by Wilson, but it is close enough to offer some basis for a comparison of the results of the procedure used here for determining police style with the way Wilson might have labeled Elyria, Columbia, and Newark in that same regard.

Taken together, the findings displayed in tables 5.4 and 5.5 uncover an interesting discrepancy. According to the simple frequency distributions displayed in table 5.4, Columbia is the most legalistic of the three cities studied here, while Elyria is the most watchmanlike; Newark falls between the two. The indices of dissimilarity essentially confirm this. In fact, they suggest that the differences among Elyria, Columbia, and Newark are essentially captured in a one-dimensional continuum of police style. The index difference between Columbia and Elyria is almost identical to the sum of the differences between

122 Styles of Urban Policing

Newark and each of them. Hence, we might plausibly place Columbia at the legalist pole of such a continuum and Elyria at the watchman pole, with Newark occupying a near-central point, a shade closer to Elyria.

That, however, is patently not the outcome when an overall style is attributed to a city based solely on its rate of police aggressiveness in seeking out and handling traffic affairs. Comparing the traffic incidence rates for Elyria, Columbia and Newark with those for Wilson's eight study sites, as displayed in table 5.5, Columbia would clearly be labeled as a legalistic department and Elyria as a watchmanlike one, and both of these labels would concur with those generated by the simple frequency distributions. From the traffic aggressiveness rates, however, Newark would take on a definite watchmanlike designation; in fact, it would be the most watchmanlike agency of the three studied here. This, of course, is something rather different from the style designation suggested by the frequency distributions and dissimilarity indices; absolute positions on the style continuum and relative inter-city similarities vary from one type of analysis to the other.

What is the primary reason for the fact that these two alternative methods for developing style classifications produce such discrepant results? The answer to that question lies mainly in the different mixes of calls handled. Recall that in both Elyria and Columbia, serious crimes are relatively infrequent occurrences, amounting to 11.3 percent of the sampled cases in the former and 6.5 in the latter. By the same token, percentages of traffic incidents are common; 34.0 of the logged events in Elyria and 34.3 in Columbia are such occurrences. In Newark, however, this is far from the case. Serious crime calls constitute no less than 30.2 percent of the events sampled in that agency's dispatch log, while traffic affairs constitute a mere 9.8 percent of that same sample. The Newark police are, in fact, *more* proactive than those in Elyria and Columbia when it comes to both serious crimes (with proactivity proportions of 3.9% in Elyria, 10.4% in Columbia and 18.2% in Newark) and less serious crimes or disputes (with proactivity proportions of 6.4% in Elyria, 17.6% in Columbia and 25.3% in Newark). Neither are they by any means lax in initiating traffic incidents (with a proactivity proportion of 32.4%). They simply do significantly less traffic work than do police in the other two cities, and focus significantly more heavily on crime.

Which coding procedure is better? Focusing solely on police aggressiveness in traffic affairs surely uncovers an important manner in which police agencies differ from one another and, for that reason alone may be a fruitful research tactic for some purposes. To offer a general police style designation, however, the coding scheme developed for this study would seem to be the superior option. While it is no less sensitive to police proactivity as a dimension of style, it includes information about important events in addition to traffic calls—events which are in their own right revealing of police stylistic differences. This is important; Wilson suggests that traffic aggressiveness and other types of police legalism may not correlate as well as they should if they indeed measure the same concept.[5] The measurement routine developed here uses more of the relevant information, and from it presents a more realistic picture of the empirical mix of types of police work.

That cities differ from one another with regard to their predominant orientation toward police service says little with regard to the way those same cities might vary internally in organizing police work. It might again well be that citywide proportions are merely aggregates of radically different patterns of service across discrete neighborhoods, with the aggregated proportions actually distorting more than they reveal about local police work. That is admittedly not the expectation to be derived from Wilson's argument, but proponents of the situational determination of policing would anticipate such an outcome.

Figure 5.2 and table 5.6, which is based on it, put those expectations to an empirical test. The figure is a truncated triangular percentage graph, which locates each distinct neighborhood in each of Elyria, Columbia, and Newark in accordance with its own proportions of service, watchman, and legalist events.[6] The neighborhoods are, again, those originally depicted in chapter 4. Table 5.6, which accompanies figure 5.2, presents indices of dissimilarity to highlight the most and least dissimilar pairs of areas both within and between the three cities.

That neighborhoods within a city are not all of a kind with regard to their experience of police work is clear from figure 5.2. In each of the three cities of central interest here, constituent neighborhoods vary— apparently the least on the service dimension and the most on the watchmanlike aspect. Nonetheless, the predominant message contained in the figure is less individual neighborhood variation than it is

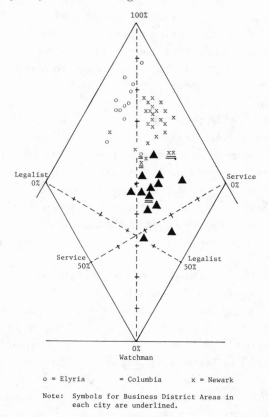

o = Elyria   ▲ = Columbia   x = Newark

Note: Symbols for Business District Areas in
each city are underlined.

Figure 5.2. The Substance of Police Work in the Neighborhoods

the essential similarity of neighborhoods within cities. In general, the
distinct neighborhoods of each of the three cities cluster together, and
at no little remove from the clusters of the others. Table 5.6 offers
some descriptive statistical backing for this contention. Interarea similarities are uniformly at their greatest among the neighborhoods of
any given city, rather than across the neighborhoods of different cities.
The continuum of city-level police styles noted earlier is not affected
by this analysis; Columbia remains the most legalistic of these three
police agencies and Elyria the most watchmanlike, with Newark hold-
ing a middle ground. What figure 5.2 and table 5.6 reveal is that these
city-level positions are not statistical artifacts of wildly skewed distributions. To the contrary, it seems clear that policing in Columbia is
relatively legalistic because policing in its neighborhoods is legalistic,
and the same holds generally for Elyria and Newark.

Table 5.6. Intra- and Intercity Style Dissimilarities

	Elyria	Columbia	Newark
Elyria	.009 .289	.043 .440	.013 .304
Columbia	—	.003 .260	.027 .435
Newark	—	—	.010 .196

Note: In each cell, the upper entry indicates the degree of dissimilarity between the two least dissimilar neighborhoods; the lower entry indicates the degree of dissimilarity between the two most dissimilar neighborhoods.

In the earlier analysis of police aggressiveness, we discovered that an area's status as a central business district rather than a residential enclave was an important determinant of the rate of police-initiated action that it experiences. In figure 5.2, the business districts of each study site are highlighted in order to facilitate the search for a similar dynamic with regard to distributions of substantive police efforts. Such an effect exists here, but it is by no means as powerful as it was in the earlier discussion nor so uniform across cities. In both Elyria and Newark, downtown policing is more legalistic than is residential policing, and in Elyria the difference in this regard is truly striking. In Columbia, however, the central business district is virtually indistinguishable from its counterpart residential areas. In the two agencies where watchmanlike policing is the rule rather than the exception, the central business district comes to look like a world unto itself with regard to substantive police work; in the generally legalistic police department, policing the downtown is a task pretty much like that of policing any other part of the city, at least with regard to the substance of the work to be done.

Styles Across Cities:
Hypotheses and Empirical Patterns

Early in chapter 3, an inferential logic was outlined for a study of the differential effects of organizational and environmental factors in the production of police styles. That logic had two component parts, both of which were deemed critical to the making of a causal inference

from any empirical findings. If, on the one hand, between-city variations in police style were stronger than within-city variations, *and*
those between-city style variations corresponded to organizational,
and not environmental, differences between cities, then an inference
about organizational determination would be in order. If, on the other
hand, either of these conditions were not met, an inference about
environmental determination would be most appropriate from the
data at hand.

From both the city-level and the neighborhood-level patterns of
police aggressiveness and substantive police watchmanism in Elyria,
Columbia, and Newark that have been described and displayed in this
chapter, it would appear that the first of these conditions has been
met. Refinements to this analysis are in order and worth pursuing
(and they will be in the next chapter), but for now the evidence
appears relatively clear and compelling. Further, it appears relatively
clear and compelling for both police aggressiveness and substantive
workload, the two dimensions of style for which measures have been
constructed and analyzed here. Only one environmental factor has
emerged so far that generates commonality across cities and heterogeneity within them; that, of course, is the status of a local area as
being or being part of a central business district. Exclude such areas,
and the across-city heterogeneity seems only to be further magnified.

In light of this, it seems worthwhile at this point to address the
second component of the inferential logic that guides this effort. In
chapters 3 and 4, a series of hypotheses was offered to account for
intercity variations in matters that were arguably related to police
style—specifically to what was then termed "police legalism." It is
now clear that there are actually two dimensions of style for which
observed patterns can be compared to expectations derived from the
hypotheses and that, at the city level of analysis, the two are only
imperfectly associated; so some adjustments to those expectations
may be in order. Nonetheless, it seems important that we now move on
to the building of those comparisons.

Regional Location. From the analyses of both absolute and relative
urban police strength in the urban communities of Ohio, New Jersey,
and South Carolina presented in chapter 3, a regional difference
emerged to set off patterns of police allocation in South Carolina from
those typical in Ohio and New Jersey. In the Northern cities, both

absolute and relative levels of police strength in a community were at least in part structured as responses to reported crime rates; this was not the case in Columbia. The style-related inference drawn from this finding was that agencies the size of whose personnel complements were specifically responsive to reported crime rates would take a more legalistic stance in providing police service, presumably in response to the magnitude of that crime problem and the local demand for its reduction. Agencies that paid no specific heed to crime in making their staffing decisions, on the other hand, would be more watchmanlike in their styles. Because Elyria, Columbia, and Newark fit in with their respective statewide staffing patterns to a satisfactory degree, this hypothesis was extended directly to them; Columbia was anticipated to be the least aggressive and most watchmanlike of the three police agencies, while Elyria's and Newark's police departments were expected to be the opposite.

From the patterns of police aggressiveness and substantive police style presented in this chapter, it seems clear that no support is forthcoming for the hypothesis for a regional basis for the production of police styles. In terms of pure police aggressiveness, neither Columbia nor Elyria demonstrate the levels anticipated for them; police are too aggressive in the former and not sufficiently so in the latter to allow the regional hypothesis to stand. For traffic aggressiveness, the results are even more disconfirming; working with this measure alone, the empirical results fall exactly opposite the expectations hypothesized for them. On this measure, Columbia is the *most* aggressive agency, and Elyria and Newark are the *least*. The same lack of confirmation holds with regard to the distributions of police activities by substantive style types. Again, Columbia is the most legalistic agency and Elyria the least, with Newark falling about in the middle. Regional differences of the kind outlined in chapter 3 simply and completely fail to account for these empirical patterns. While neither this nor any other hypothesis can be adequately "tested" by a mere three cases, the findings from these analyses are sufficiently strong and consistent to suggest that the regional hypothesis is open to a good deal of doubt as an explanation for variations in the most salient dimensions of police style.

Information Systems and Institution-Building. In chapter 4 a hypothesis was developed linking the quality of data offered by dispatch

systems to police legalism. Recall that in terms of technological sophistication, the continuum of cities that emerged from the discussion
placed Newark at the top, Columbia in the middle, and Elyria at the
bottom. In terms of organizational adaptation to that sophistication—
what Janowitz (1969) has called the process of internal institution-
building—the pattern was a bit different. Unsurprisingly enough, the
more sophisticated systems generated and retained more information
than their less sophisticated counterparts; nonetheless, as indicated
by the quality of the data on police action in each city, Newark and
Elyria appear best adapted to their respective information systems,
and Columbia least adapted to its. The hypothesis constructed from
these differences was one based on policy assumptions and concerns
common among law enforcement professionals; specifically, that hypothesis suggested that legalistic policing would be dependent on the
degree of adaptation a police department makes to its information
coding and retrieving system. From that hypothesis, it was anticipated
that the most aggressive and legalistic policing would emerge in Newark, with Elyria falling somewhat behind Newark in these regards.
Columbia was anticipated in the best case to equal Elyria in aggressiveness and legalism, but in the more realistic case to fall below it
and manifest the least aggressive and legalistic styles of policing.

Once again, these hypotheses go unconfirmed by the empirical
results uncovered in this chapter, and the lack of congruence here is
even more severe than it was for the regional hypothesis. Columbia's
police are neither least aggressive nor least legalistic; the Elyria police
department is not a middle-range agency on either of these dimensions of police action; police in Newark are aggressive, but not overly
legalistic. Focusing on traffic aggressiveness does nothing to salvage
this hypothesis. From the data analyzed here, it would appear that the
availability, quality, and use of activity information in urban police
departments is generally unrelated to the kind of action they under-
take in their service environments. Policies based on the contrary
assumption would seem highly questionable, and the program efforts
they spawn might well prove a waste of time and effort.

***Urbanization, Governmental Form, and Police Organizational
Structure.*** From the analyses of urban arrest rates that were presented in chapter 2 for a national sample of American cities, a set of

hypotheses about the legalistic police style were developed. The key predictor variables in that set were the span of supervisory control—specifically the officer/sergeant ratio—characteristic of a police department, the form of government in the city served by that department, the degree of civilianization characteristic of the policy agency, and the degree of urbanization characteristic of the larger city itself. Empirical results for each of these and the implications of those results for their guiding hypotheses deserve an extended word.

Police Agency Size, Span of Control, and Officer Discretion. From the results of his study of police discretion in the Los Angeles area, Michael Brown (1981) offers a hypothesis relating the structures of police organizations to the actions taken and the attitudes held by their individual patrol officers. In his discussion, Brown attempts to relate the size of a police agency with the exercise of discretion by its members. His treatment actually begins with neither of these variables, however, but rather with the notion of police professionalization and the movement to bring it about that has swept American police departments (Caiden 1977). Centralization, one of the keystones of that movement, is basic to Brown's hypothesis. By means of increased centralization in police departments, individual patrol officers are supposedly made more responsive in the conduct of their work to organizational dictates mediated through the commands of superior officers and field supervisors, and correspondingly less responsive to the demands or requests coming from individuals and groups in the communities those officers serve. At the same time, in more centralized departments officers also become more responsive to the expectations of their patrol colleagues and to the general culture of policing. In either event, the contemporary police professionalization movement effectively insulates police officers and their departments from the norms of community life, which might otherwise guide their actions while on duty. Instead, it immerses them in the norms of organizational and occupational life. (For some empirical corroboration on this point, see Slovak 1983.)

It is here where police department size comes into play. In large agencies, patrol officers receive less direction and control from their immediate supervisors, usually patrol sergeants,[7] so that more room is left the patrol officers for the exercise of discretion than is true of their counterparts in smaller agencies. Conversely, in smaller agencies, patrol sergeants can more closely monitor the work of their officers and can—by design or inadvertently—constrain them from acting independently, experimentally, or in any other way that might prove threatening to the sergeant's authority. Thus, Brown's argument is that in a situation where police agencies pursue "professionalism" and experience the insulation from their communities attendant upon it, department size and police discretion will be positively related. The analyses offered in chapter 2—and, specifically, the finding that there is a positive link between a broad span of control, the officer's broadened discretion that can be presumed to flow from that, and the making of more "legalistic" arrests for violent crimes—provide some empirical corroboration for at least part of this argument. It therefore deserves a detailed analysis in the context of police style in our three cities.

It is worth noting that Brown uses primarily attitudinal data collected from working police officers in the city and suburbs of Los Angeles to develop his argument in a convincing manner. No comparable attitudinal data were collected for this effort, but some of the materials culled from dispatch logs are related to the idea of police discretion and, especially, to the legalistic police style. Brown's logic is most directly embodied in the measure of police aggressiveness developed here; it and the empirical findings presented in chapter 2 suggest that Newark will be policed most aggressively and Elyria least, with Columbia falling somewhere in between. Brown does not treat substantive police style in anything like the terms used here, so the data on that aspect of local policing do not fit well with his hypothesis. Nonetheless, legalistic policing in this study is by definition police-initiated; thus, the same continuum of agencies might be anticipated here with regard to the relative legalism contained in their respective workloads.

The analyses presented in chapter 2 demonstrated for the 42 cities studied there a clear positive relationship between police department size and supervisory span of control, such that on the average the larger agencies allocated more patrol officers to any given sergeant than did their smaller counterparts. As depicted in the first panel of figure 5.3, the size-span positive association also holds across our three cities.[8] From the empirical patterns generated and displayed in this chapter, there is no support for the hypothesis of a relationship between substantive police legalism and either police agency size or

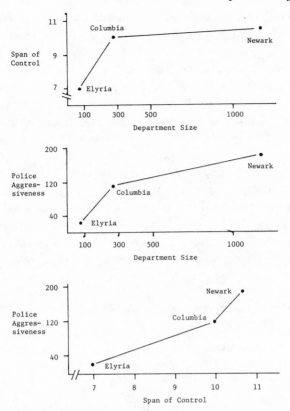

Figure 5.3. Police Aggressiveness, Police Department Size, and Supervisory Span of Control

supervisory span of control, but again that is probably not the best test of Brown's argument. Pure police aggressiveness is a preferable measure for that purpose, and for it that support emerges. In fact, empirical relationships emerge to link aggressiveness to both agency size and span of control, and in both cases these relationships are in the anticipated positive direction. These are displayed in the second and third panels of figure 5.3. The former is nearly logarithmic in form, suggesting the existence of a natural "ceiling" on the degree to which a large police department can encourage or allow the street-level discretion that leads to aggressive policing. The latter is more nearly linear, as is only to be expected from the hypothesis. Be that as it may, these constitute the first set of findings that support a hypothesis about intercity differences on the dimensions of police style addressed in this chapter. It bears noting, in addition, that the hypothesis supported is an organizational rather than an environmental one.[9]

Command Structures and Political Connections. A fourth hypothesis that is "testable" with the data at hand is the one that emerges from the findings reported in chapter 2 that higher arrest rates, and thus presumably a more legalistic form of policing, are registered in cities administered by appointed city managers rather than elected mayors. This finding by itself stands as confirmation for a hypothesis put forward some time ago by Bordua and Reiss (1966) who sought to develop a typology of police organizational command systems based on the relative security of the tenure of the police chief and whether the relation of the chief to the mayor was more one of "strict accountability" or "feudal allegiance." Bordua and Reiss did not specifically or systematically tie police working styles to these command system types, but they hinted at such connections:

Perhaps, in the long run, it is hard to have a professionalized police without a professionalized mayor. Perhaps, also, this would lead us to expect different kinds of command styles when a professional city manager intervenes between the chief and the mayor. If the civil superior, for whatever reason, does not demand accountability from the chief, the quasi-formalized obsession with "command" as a principle of control may be replaced by a complex system of feudal loyalties. In this situation, ties of personal political fealty between chief and mayor—or between chief and the local "powers"—may become prominent and "keep your nose clean" the principle of subordination.

This last sounds notably like the watchman style of policing. Further, it sounds in their treatment like a police style to be anticipated where appointed chiefs report directly to elected mayors. By extension, more legalistic policing might be anticipated where chiefs report to appointed city managers, themselves a product of the good-government, bureaucratic approach to public service in American cities.[10]

How does this suggestion apply to policing in our cities? In Columbia, as noted in chapter 3, the police chief reports to an appointed city manager who, in turn, is responsible to the city's elected council and its mayor. From Bordua and Reiss' discussion and from the findings displayed in chapter 2, we would anticipate police work in that city to be particularly aggressive and legalistic. On the other hand, in Elyria and in Newark the police executive is directly responsible to and appointed by the city's elected mayor; in both, those police executives have historically played active roles in mayoral election campaigns. In each, then, less aggressive and more watchmanlike styles might be anticipated.

The only way that the patterns of police aggressiveness discussed in this chapter can be made consistent with the expectation derived from Bordua and Reiss' discussion is if the focus is limited solely to the rate of police-initiated traffic incidents, where such consistency does indeed emerge. For any other measure of aggressiveness, and especially for the purer version used for the other hypothesis tests reported thus far, such is not the case. All things considered, we are on relatively shaky ground in attributing a determining role for police aggressiveness to the connections between police chiefs and political structures. With regard to substantive police style, however, the hypothesized patterns are generally quite congruent with those actually observed in the data. Columbia indeed has the most legalistic police agency of those studied here; it is also the only one of these three cities administered by an appointed city manager. Elyria's is the most watchmanlike police department, and it offers a direct mayor-chief administrative pattern. Newark, served by a middle-ground agency in terms of legalism and watchmanlike policing, is in fact organized for police administration with an elected mayor overseeing an appointed police director who in turn oversees a police chief with responsibility for daily police operations. Compared to Columbia and Elyria, at least, this "mixed" structure produces a "mixed" police style, buttressing further the explanatory power of the Bordua-Reiss hypothesis.

Civilianization. In the analyses reported in chapter 2, strong positive links emerged between arrest rates for offenses against both persons and property and the degree to which a police department's personnel complement is composed of civilian employees. From those findings, another hypothesis on police style was offered, namely: that agencies with larger civilian staff components should be enabled to shift more officers from organizational maintenance tasks to patrol or crime-fighting assignments, and thus should be expected to register higher levels of police aggressiveness and substantive police legalism in the work that they do.

At the times the data for this research were collected, the Elyria, Columbia, and Newark police departments registered civilianization percentages of 10.5, 23.2 and 21.8, respectively, marking the first as low, the second as high and third as relatively high on a continuum of civilianization. Positions on this continuum obviously bear little resemblance to the degrees of pure police aggressiveness displayed in the three cities, but they do correspond rather well to degrees of substantive police legalism. The Newark police department probably registers a bit less legalism than it should, given its relatively high proportion of civilian employees, but Columbia and Elyria emerge as expected with regard to this relationship. For that matter, Newark's actual position in this association is not all that far from its anticipated status. Thus, another organizational hypothesis about the determination of local police styles seems at least partially confirmed by these data.

Urbanization. The sixth and final hypothesis about intercity variations in police style to be tested here comes from the finding, produced in chapter 2, that arrest rates for both property- and violence-related serious crimes are direct, strong, and positive functions of "urbanization." In that analysis, urbanization was created statistically as one factor or dimension composed primarily of city population size, percentage of the city population that is black, and reported crime rates. There is good theoretical reason to expect that hypothesis to hold with regard to the dimensions of police style in our cities, for, as Black (1976) has argued, self-starting agents of formal social control—like aggressive, legalistic police officers—must fill the gap left when the vehicles for informal control are attenuated or are absent altogether. The latter is far more likely, of course, in a larger than in a smaller city.

On urbanization as a composite index or on any of its specific components as listed above, the cities studied here fall consistently along an urbanization continuum such that Newark scores high and Elyria low, with Columbia in between. That pattern is generally not replicated for scores on substantive police legalism across those same cities, but it aligns quite nicely with their respective levels of pure police aggressiveness. The only matter at issue in this regard is whether this urbanization effect on police aggressiveness is best thought a direct or an indirect one. One of the clearest lessons forthcoming from the analyses of absolute police strength offered in chapter 3 was that city size heavily determines police department size; as we have seen above in figure 5.3, the latter in turn structures supervisory span of control which, in its own turn, structures police aggressiveness. The urbanization effect identified here may well be an indirect one, working through these other organizational characteristics. In any event, the hypothesis seems confirmed with regard to police aggressiveness, but not with substantive legalism.

Conclusions

From the data culled from the police dispatch logs, we have in this chapter created and analyzed measures of two dimensions of police style: police aggressiveness and the substantive content of police work. From a reassessment of Wilson's discussion, these measures appear to capture what is most salient in the general concept of a police style, with the added advantage that they facilitate comparisons both within and across cities. That advantage is by no means trivial. The analyses of substantive police workload and aggressiveness conducted here make it quite clear not only that the style of police work varies from one city to the next, but also that police styles vary somewhat within a given city as well, depending on the kind of neighborhood—downtown business or residential—in which they are enacted.

Within the limits posed by having only three cases at our disposal, we have also now "tested" six hypotheses about variations in the dimensions of police styles. The results of those testing exercises are summarized in table 5.7. Included also in that table are the findings on the link between the business/residential status of a neighborhood and the relative aggressiveness of the police work it experiences, which emerged from the analyses offered in this chapter even though it was not the subject of an explicit hypothesis. There is much here to support an argument for the importance of the police organization and its dynamics in generating various kinds of police action, and much less to support an environmental or situational explanation as an alternative. Of course, to pose the matter in such stark, either/or terms is to overstate the case. Whether a neighborhood is a residential community or a part of the city's central business district is clearly an environmental dichotomy, and one which structures local police aggressiveness; similarly, the degree of urbanization characteristic of a

Table 5.7. Summary of "Test" Results of Hypotheses on Police Style

Hypothesis:	Dimension of Police Style	
	"Pure" Police Aggressiveness	*Relative Level of Legalistic Police Work*
Regionalism	Not Supported	Not Supported
Information systems and institution-building	Not Supported	Not Supported
CBD status of area	Supported	Not Supported
Urbanization	Supported[a]	Not Supported
Police agency size, span of control, and officer discretion	Supported	Not Supported[b]
Command systems and political connections	Not Supported	Supported
Police Civilianization	Not Supported	Supported

[a] But arguably an indirect effect.
[b] But arguably not an appropriate test measure.

community is also an environmental affair, and it structures the degree of local police aggressiveness as well, albeit probably in an indirect way. Granting that, however, it appears that police agency size and supervisory span of control—and especially the latter—are "prime movers" in the police aggressiveness story, while the kinds of connections forged between police and city executives and the degree of civilianization a police department has undergone appear to play the same role for substantive police legalism. These results, when combined with the patterns noted earlier of general intracity homogeneity and intercity heterogeneity on police aggressiveness and legalism, are more consistent with an argument for generation of police style based on the dynamics of police organizations. We might depict that argument graphically, in figure 5.4, as a causal argument in which the structure of the police agency mediates between some very general characteristics of the policing environment and the specific dimen-

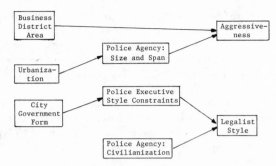

Figure 5.4. The Production of Police Style: A Tentative Model

sions of police action, to break up the mechanistic cause-and-effect argument that often characterizes environmental or ecological theories of police work.

Notes

1. Despite his own later reliance on traffic citation rates, Wilson explicitly noted in the original treatment of the legalistic style that traffic enforcement policy is highly malleable. High citation rates are often temporary phenomena produced by departments needing to justify themselves to skeptical administrators and publics. They can equally well be produced by protesting police unions. Excluding such rates from a measure of style may in fact be a more advisable course than relying solely on them for that measure.

2. Police personnel—civilian and sworn officers together—per thousand city residents, as of the 1980 U.S. Census.

3. We cannot account for the remaining area in Columbia on any systematic basis, but it is worth noting that this neighborhood abuts the state hospital for the mentally ill. That may account for some—albeit probably not all— of its unusually high rate of police aggressiveness.

4. By way of reminder, all administrative or organizational maintenance events were eliminated from these analyses, due to their irrelevance to both the Wilson typology and our substantive concerns here.

5. Across the seven cases in his original study for which data were available, the correlation between the traffic ticket index and that for drunk arrests per 1000 population—both arguably good indicators of police legalism— was a mere rho = .32.

6. To derive these percentages, we simply cross tabulated calls on the basis of both their style designations and the areas in which they occurred. This, of

course, causes us to lose cases in each city. In each case, however, most of the cases so lost were service-oriented matters, testifying rather eloquently to the priority placed in these three cities and in American policing generally on the "real" police work generated by crime and disorder. In any event, the effect of this cross tabulation is to make our cities appear even less service-oriented than in table 5.4.

7. There is nothing unique to police in this contention. To the contrary, that size leads to lower levels of "administrative intensity" is a standard finding produced by sociological studies of organizations of all types. For verification on this point, see Rushing (1967), Pondy (1969) or Blau and Schoenherr (1974).

8. The value for Newark's span of control used in the graphs in figure 5.3 is the result of dividing all officers and detectives by the total number of police sergeants. The detectives are included in the numerator because some of the sergeants are detective sergeants, and because some detectives and some detective sergeants engage in regular, undercover patrols of Newark's streets and beats.

9. Recall that absolute police strength is predominantly a function of city size in all three states containing one of our study sites. Relative police strength, on the other hand, is not so easily attributable to a single, environmental phenomenon. Both, however, exhibit the pattern suggested by Brown's argument; hence the contention about the organizational nature of this explanation.

10. That such political structures have definite effects on local spending policies and patterns of resource allocation and conflict resolution in American cities is a well-documented empirical finding. See Clark (1968) or Hawley (1975) for evidence in this regard. Hawley's treatment is particularly telling when we attempt to transport the logic of "professional" government to police policy and style matters.

6. The Ecologies of Urban Police Styles

The development of a "style strategy" for the provision of urban police services seems, from what has been said thus far in this work, to be a politico-organizational process. The particular strategy chosen varies in its major dimensions from city to city, but the choice itself is one tailored to both police organizational realities and demands and to the service-provision philosophies—which some might call ideologies—of local political leaders and urban administrators. The choice might well be, in addition, a response to local environmental conditions and variations. One of those conditions, as we have seen from the studies of policing in Elyria, Columbia and Newark, is the status of an urban neighborhood as either a residential enclave or a constituent part of the central business district. Nonetheless, more is at stake in the environmental argument. In any given city or "urban mosaic" (Timms 1971), neighborhoods typically differ from one another on demographic, social, economic, and a host of other grounds. In doing so, they differ in terms of the rhythms and patterns of the social life they contain and of the norms of interactional order which guide that life. Police officers and executives alike are well aware of this. Do they, as a result, tailor a style strategy to account for it? Are the strategies so tailored identical, or even generally comparable, across cities?

To ask the first question is to ask whether police styles are structured situationally to any significant degree in any given city; to ask the second is to ask whether the bases of such situationalism are general or generalizable across cities. It is fair to raise such questions here, for the analyses of police style presented thus far have not directly faced this most sophisticated version of the argument for the environmental determination of police work. No alternative argument based on politico-organizational factors can stand until that is done.

The purpose of this last analytical chapter is to raise these situational questions about police style and to answer them from the data for Elyria, Columbia and Newark. While the analyses presented in chapter 5 showed that variations in the dimensions of police style are a good deal larger across than within these cities, it certainly did not show that variations of the latter type are nonexistent. That they do occur, and that they occur among the non-business-district areas in each city, makes it realistic to search these data for environmental correlates of police style. That search and the results it produces will fully and finally round out this study of "organization versus environment" in the context of urban policing.

Cases and Measures

The analytic strategy for the presentations that follow is a mirror image of that which was used in chapter 4. After defining and describing the empirical measures of both police style and neighborhood character on which the analysis is based, the narrative proceeds through a serial discussion of the ecology of police work in Elyria, in Columbia, and in Newark. It closes with a comparative assessment that analyzes all three simultaneously. Throughout, the units of analysis are the neighborhood areas in each city defined by aggregating police beats and census tracts until they come into perfect or near contiguity, and depicted in the maps in chapter 4. These same areas were, of course, the units of analysis for the research presented in the prior chapter.

Measures of Police Style. For empirical indicators of the major dimensions of local police style, two specific measures will be employed. The first of these is the percentage of a neighborhood's police calls that are watchmanlike (with the latter defined here in accord with the analysis offered in chapter 5). This measure of substantive police style is preferable to an alternative tapping legalism because on it, and not the alternative, emerges the widest range of variations among neighborhoods both within and across the three cities (see figure 5.2.).[1] The second measure of police style is familiar from the analysis offered in chapter 5: it is the rate of police-initiated intrusiveness into neighborhood life, exclusive of traffic-related incidents. This measure is calculated and reported on an annual basis, per thousand residents of a given neighborhood area.

Measures of Neighborhood Character. The measures of neighborhood character to be used in this analysis are drawn from the tract-level data reported in the 1970 U.S. Census for Elyria, Columbia and Newark, and are then aggregated as necessary to correspond to the actual neighborhoods defined for this study. The decision to use 1970 data on neighborhood character requires something of an extended discussion, for it is probably a less than ideal procedure. The research assumption that social geography structures police action is, in effect, an assumption that a territory which contains given types, numbers, and distributions of people will consistently offer the same types of interactions and situations to patrol officers, who will in turn respond to those in a generally similar fashion. There is, of course, a temporal process embedded in this presumption. Patrol officers must learn the ecologies of their beats in order to learn of likely situations to be encountered and of the variety of acceptable or problematic responses they might offer. Such learning, in most American police departments, is acquired not through lectures or study in the police academy but rather through first-hand experience, and such experience takes time to acquire. Ideally, then, the measures of neighborhood character for a study like this would predate those of police action by the appropriate amount of time necessary for the acquisition of ecological knowledge by the police. The relevant time lapse here probably varies with the size of the beat to be patrolled and the assignment practices and beat-rotation procedures of the police department. Nonetheless, a four- or five-year lapse would not be implausible. Since the data available span altogether the 1978–81 period, the ideal collection of neighborhood data for our cities would cover approximately 1975. Of course, no such information exists. We are, of necessity, thrown back to the most recent prior collections of area data for these cities, the 1970 Census.

What are the implications of this? Given that the character and composition of a census tract can change over almost any reasonable period of time, research findings that tie area character to police action over a ten-year span will, if anything, understate "real" relationships. From what other scholars have discovered about patterns of neighborhood change, however, the degree of understatement is likely to be small. The most pertinent empirical evidence on this point is that offered by Albert Hunter (1974), who studied patterns of demographic, social, and economic change in Chicago's 75 community areas, using data from the four censuses from 1930 to 1960. "Community areas" in Chicago are similar to the neighborhood areas defined here, in that both are aggregations of census tracts. One of the major points of Hunter's analysis was the relatively low likelihood (on the average, amounting to a probability of roughly .20) of a community's undergoing any notable change over the period that he studied. The use of 1970 data in this research is still a compromise with what would be an ideal procedure, but Hunter's results suggest that it may not be all that compromising after all.

Selection of specific census-based measures for the neighborhoods of interest was guided less by the literature of studies on police and more by that in the field of urban ecology. Ever since at least the 1920s, ecologists have sought to uncover the primary or basic dimensions differentiating urban neighborhoods from one another. The results of their research have tended to converge around a general consensus. In the United States, and in some other areas of the world as well (Berry 1972), the city as an ecological entity is apparently best conceived as three cities in one. It is, first, a city of *socioeconomic status* differentials, in which persons of similar status cluster together in different sectors of the local geography. As a whole, the socio-economic city is a collection of pie-shaped sectors, each of which contains a population at a relatively common status level. Secondly, the city is a collection of areas differentiated by the stage in the *family life-cycle* through which their residents are passing. This "familistic" city is a concentric zonal affair, with neighborhoods becoming more so—that is, with ever larger proportions of their households occupied by two married adults raising young children at home in single-family dwelling units, with women engaged primarily as homemakers—with their increasing distance from the city center. Finally, the city is a collection of *racial and ethnic groups*, whose members cluster to-gether, voluntarily or involuntarily, in given neighborhoods spread over the general urban ecology in a multinucleated pattern.

There is no good reason on the surface to expect our cities to vary notably from this typical pattern. With regard to Newark, in fact, there is empirical evidence of its general conformity in this regard (Janson 1968). Thus, measuring for Elyria, Columbia and Newark the specific variables that constitute these three general dimensions of urban differentiation should capture the most salient features of their respective urban environments, those most likely to pose the differing immediate contexts in which police work is carried out. Accordingly, the following measures were collected for each neighborhood area included in this analysis:

1. Median income of families and unrelated individuals;
2. Median years of schooling completed by the population aged 25 or older;
3. Median value of the owner-occupied housing units;
4. Percent of the working population employed in professional or technical pursuits;
5. Percent of the population aged 5 or younger;
6. Percent of the adult population (aged 14 or older) that is married;
7. Percent of the adult (i.e., aged 14 or older) women that are employed;
8. Percent of the dwelling units that are owner-occupied;
9. Percent of the population that is black;
10. Percent of the population that is foreign-born.

These measures have appeared in many ecological studies and are, in fact, a virtual duplicate of the list of variables used by Hunter (1974). In accordance with the findings produced by him and by other urban ecologists, it seems reasonable to anticipate that in our cities variables 1 through 4 will cluster into one dimension of socioeconomic status; that variables 5 through 8 will cluster into a dimension of familism; and that variables 9 and 10 will compose a racial-ethnic dimension. To the extent that any of these basic dimensions of urban differentiation produce consistent patterns of police action, the variables that compose each should relate in similar fashion to the measures of police style being examined.

For this analysis, four other measures were collected for each neighborhood as well:

11. Percent of the population aged 65 and older;
12. Percent of the population between 15 and 19 years of age;
13. Household density;
14. Percent of the population living in the same dwelling they occupied five years earlier.

From the standpoint of urban ecological research, all four are logically indicators of familism[2] and, where they have been included in empirical studies, have usually performed as such. They are included here, however, because each has also made an appearance—albeit sometimes rather indirectly—in studies of or relevant to the topic of police performance. Research on fear of crime (Phillips and Politzer 1982) suggests that the urban elderly are particularly afflicted with a sense of personal insecurity and might therefore prove particularly vocal in demanding police protection. Similarly, teenagers in their generational revolt against authority figures might as a result become magnets for police attention and action. Density has long been theorized by sociologists of the city to be a sufficient, and sometimes even a necessary, cause of the rise of various urban pathologies, among them crime (Wirth 1938); sophisticated empirical research on this topic has uncovered household density as the special culprit in this regard (Galle, Gove and McPherson 1972). Finally, studies of police patrol work have often noted the way immediate police attention is focused, in any given neighborhood context, on the unusal or the different. The measure of residential immobility gathered for this research is intended as a negative indicator of this, tapping one dimension of stability or a lack of change in a local community.

What should we hypothesize specifically about the link between neighborhood character and police action? There is no solid lead to follow from the research of others in this regard, for almost no serious efforts to tie ecological variations within a city to police patterns in particular or to social control efforts in general have yet appeared. Conflict theory in sociology, however, offers a broad perspective on such matters that can be applied to this study. That body of thought suggests that those who monopolize or at least possess significant amounts of socially relevant resources will exert social control over those lacking such resources (Collins 1975). Donald Black (1976) has used this perspective to bring together in one coherent treatment many of the separate studies of law in action that dot the literature. Further, as was noted in chapters 2 and 3, Allan Liska and Mitchell Chamlin (1984) and David Jacobs (1979), among others, have all used variants of conflict theory to explain the relationships their empirical studies uncovered between various city characteristics and police strength, urban arrest rates, and other police-relevant matters. A fair guiding hypothesis for this effort, borrowing from their work, would suggest that to the extent environmental variations structure police action, it will be resourceful neighborhoods—those populated by upper-status, familistic, native white persons—who will demand that social control be exerted over their lower-status, non-familistic, black and foreign-born counterparts. It is in the neighborhoods of the latter where the highest levels of police aggressiveness, proactivity, and stylistic legalism might be anticipated.

Elyria

Because only twelve neighborhood areas in Elyria were defined by means of the beat/tract aggregration procedure, there is relatively little that can be reliably said about the ecological distribution of population groupings across the town's social space, at least not in terms of the sectors, zones, or multinucleated clusters so familiar in ecological theory. It is worth noting, however, that amid some variations, the "average" Elyria neighborhood for purposes of this analysis is relatively middle-class. Its population is generally white, married, of middle-income status, home-owning and moderately educated, as the summary statistics displayed in table 6.1 affirm. It is also notable that, by and large, these characteristics cluster statistically in ways generally predicted by ecological theory. Table 6.2 presents the results to support this contention, in the form of factor-loadings and commu-

Table 6.1. The Character of Elyria's Neighborhoods

	Descriptive Statistics	
Variable		*Standard*
(N = 12)	*Mean*	*Deviation*
Percent Black	11.1	13.9
Percent Children	10.1	2.5
Median Income	$10,461	$1,384
Percent Elderly	9.3	5.0
Percent Teen-agers	8.9	0.8
Percent Married	65.2	7.3
Percent Foreign-born	2.3	0.9
Median School Years Completed	11.6	0.9
Percent Residentially Immobile	49.8	10.4
Percent Professionals	11.0	5.4
Percent Working Women	39.5	4.0
Household Density	3.2	0.4
Median Value of Homes	$16,979	$5,459
Percent Owner-Occupied Homes	63.8	20.7

Table 6.2. Factor Loadings and Communalities in Elyria

	Factor Loadings			
Variables	1	2	3	Communality
Blacks	−.808	.140	.346	.792
Children	−.487	.737	−.290	.863
Income	.872	.282	.195	.878
Elderly	−.120	−.987	−.066	.991
Teenagers	−.102	−.140	.982	.995
Married	.607	.770	.093	.971
Foreign-born	.206	.173	.522	.345
Schooling	.908	.027	−.177	.856
Residential Stability	.482	.084	.118	.253
Professionals	.833	−.148	.070	.721
Working Women	−.139	.699	−.005	.507
Density	.166	.892	.129	.840
Home Values	.781	−.035	.248	.673
Owner-Occupancy	.734	.541	.319	.933
% Variance Explained	40.6	26.2	13.1	

nality indices from a principal components, orthogonal-rotation factor analysis[3] that included all fourteen of the measures of neighborhood character.

In Elyria, racial-ethnic composition is not a strong dimension of neighborhood differentiation, but socioeconomic status and stage in the family life-cycle most definitely are. The former in Elyria is a dimension the high end of which is composed of high levels of education and income, high rates of professional occupations and owner-occupied homes which are themselves of high value, and small proportions of blacks. There is also in these data some indication of a positive correlation between residential immobility and socioeconomic status, although this is clearly a secondary factor in the production of the status dimension. Stage in the family life-cycle clusters high proportions of married adults, young children, and working women, with high levels of household density and low proportions of the elderly. Note in this regard that the proportion of working women, while it clusters well with these other variables, does so positively rather than negatively. In Elyria (but not only in Elyria, as will become apparent below) familism is coming to mean a working rather than a home-making female adult. Finally, a third dimension of differentiation emerges from the analysis to link high proportions of teenagers and the foreign-born. Note from the communality indices included in table 6.2 that the foreign-born measure is an exceedingly weak contributor to this factor; for all practical purposes, this last is a dimension purely and simply of teenagers in the local population.

Pure police agressiveness and a substantively watchmanlike police workload, the two dimensions of police style of interest here, both vary rather widely across the twelve neighborhoods of Elyria, more widely in fact than many of the social and demographic measures of neighborhood character. On the average, 74.5 percent of an Elyria neighborhood's calls for police service are for watchmanlike events, but this mean value masks an actual range of variation in watchmanlike percentages between a low of 59 and a high of 88 percent. By the same token, the average Elyria neighborhood experiences a nontraffic police aggressiveness rate of 30.5 incidents per thousand population per year, but the actual range spans low and high values of 6.6 and 159.3 incidents. Some of this variation, of course, is generated by the peculiarities of policing in Elyria's central business district, where the watchman proportion is lower and the police aggressiveness level is higher than they are anywhere else in town. Excluding the downtown, the average area of Elyria has 75.9 percent of its calls for service fall into the watchman category, and experiences 18.8 police-initiated nontraffic incidents per 1000 population per year. It is also worth noting that police aggressiveness and a heavily watchmanlike police workload are empirically related to a high degree across the internal areas of Elyria. In general, the more intrusive police are in a neighborhood's life, the less the proportion of watchmanlike calls in that area's police workload ($r = -.766$). Further, this holds despite the special nature of downtown policing, for the intrusiveness-watchman correlation shrinks only minimally ($r = -.709$) when the central business district is excluded from its calculation. These findings are not surprising; aggressive policing of a watchmanlike nature seems intuitively a severe contradiction in terms. Nonetheless, it is worth recalling that this result is not methodologically predetermined. In these data, as in those for Columbia and Newark to be addressed below, it is possible for a relatively watchmanlike area to see a relatively high police aggressiveness rate, depending on its population size. In Elyria, however, the two almost never go together; to the contrary, more of one rather invariably means less of the other.

Is there an identifiable ecological basis to variations in police aggressiveness and in relatively watchmanlike police work across the neighborhoods of Elyria? Table 6.3 provides the evidence needed to answer that question. In the table, the social and demographic measures of neighborhood character are grouped in accordance with their clustering about the more general ecological factors displayed earlier; within each grouping, variables are listed in accordance with the magnitude of their original loadings on those factors, from the strongest to the weakest. The two left-hand columns of coefficients are based on all twelve of Elyria's neighborhood areas; the two on the right exclude the central business district, and thus are based on the remaining eleven areas.

There lies, in the findings displayed in table 6.3, no easy answer to the question of an environmental basis for the major dimensions of police style. Rather, there emerges a complicated picture which requires detailed decomposition and analysis. That, in itself, says something. That coefficients vary in magnitude and direction within ecological clusters of variables and depending on the inclusion or exclusion of the central business district suggests that police work in Elyria is not so easily understood as a simple function of urban ecological differentiation. If policing in Elyria is strategically carried out as a response to neighborhood-level variations, the strategy appears to be based in relatively specific environmental contingencies and may be idiosyncratic to that city. It will require comparative analysis to see whether that is in fact the case, but the possibility is definitely open.

As we noted earlier, the central business district in Elyria is a peculiarly nonwatchmanlike, proactive police area compared with its counterparts. It is also peculiar socially and demographically, containing a disproportionately poor, renting, unmarried, and uneducated population. That fact is borne out in a comparison of the differences between correlations in the left and right hand panels of table 6.3. In that the right-hand panel offers a more controlled picture of the environment's effects on the styles of local police work in Elyria, we will focus on it in the discussion to follow.

For one who would argue that police style in Elyria is environmentally determined, table 6.3 is relatively disappointing. Only 5 of the 28 coefficients in the right-hand panel of the table manage to fall

Table 6.3. Ecological Correlates of Police Action in Elyria

Neighborhood Measures	All Areas (N = 12)		Residential Areas (N = 11)	
	Police Aggres- siveness	Relative Watch- manism	Police Aggres- siveness	Relative Watch- manism
I. Socioeconomic Status				
Schooling	-.478	.456	-.028	.216
Income	-.281	.115	.008	-.095
Professionals	-.322	.382	-.165	.271
Blacks	.153	-.094	-.125	.042
Home Values	-.130	-.096	.474	-.366
Owner-Occupancy	-.560	.198	.298	-.365
Immobility	-.342	.262	-.411	.157
II. Stage in the Family Life-Cycle				
Elderly	.394	-.027	.010	.321
Density	-.679	.386	-.148	-.063
Married	-.574	.139	.299	-.491
Children	-.212	.100	-.150	-.010
Working Women	-.245	-.109	.239	-.428
III. Teenagers				
Teenagers	-.272	.072	-.043	-.130
Foreign-Born	-.298	-.112	.031	-.423

above .4 or below −.4; relaxing the standard to ±.3 adds only three more coefficients worth noting. If we demand that a measure of neighborhood character correlate with *both* the dimensions of police style at a level of at least ±.2—a reasonable criterion in light of the strong correlation between aggressiveness and watchmanlike police work, as noted above—then there are only four variables worth examining. Two of those are measures of socioeconomic status: median home values and the percentages of owner-occupied housing. The other two, both measures of familism, are the percentages of married adults and of working women resident in an area. All four, taken together, lead to the same empirical conclusion: high status and familistic residential areas in Elyria tend to experience less watchmanlike and more aggressive police work than do their counterpart neighborhoods.

At first glance, this seems somewhat surprising; it stands in rather

direct contradiction to the expectations for such correlates that were
derived earlier from the versions of conflict theory extant in the sociology of law and in social science generally. In outlining those and in
building a guiding hypothesis for this effort, we suggested that people
living in high-status, familistic areas would want proactive law enforcement not for themselves but rather for their counterparts in low-
status, less familistic areas. The central focus of such theories, after
all, is control of the resourceless by the resourceful. While the policy-
related desires of different neighborhoods' residents for themselves
and others cannot be tapped in the data at hand, the findings presented here make it clear that what different neighborhoods get by
way of police action is not what conflict theory would have predicted.

   While neither conflict theory nor situational determinism seem to
offer adequate explanations for the correlations displayed in table 6.3,
and especially for the signs of those that attain a modest magnitude,
an organizational perspective provides an important key for their interpretation. Contingency theorists of organizational behavior (e.g.,
Pfeffer and Salancik, 1978) have argued that organizations of any type
will retain the support of those they serve, and hence their own freedom of action, only if they can demonstrate "effectiveness" in the
performance of those tasks and functions for which they claim a special expertise or mandate. Private-sector organizations can point to
indicators of profitability, market share, or productivity to demonstrate their effectiveness; public-sector organizations, and certainly
most service-providing government agencies cannot do likewise. How,
then, can a police agency demonstrates its "effectiveness" to the more
influential and resource-rich elements in the community, on whom it
depends for support, especially if that agency is generally dedicated to
a reactive, watchmanlike style? One pragmatic, two-pronged strategy
for doing so would be to avoid the proactive, legalistic encounters with
the resourceless that might lead to serious confrontation and possible
disorder, while simultaneously demonstrating to the resourceful a sufficient level of police presence in their neighborhoods to assure them
of police vigilance. Perhaps this is something of a shell game, but it is
nonetheless a particularly rational strategy from the perspective of a
watchmanlike police agency. The more sizable correlations displayed
in table 6.3 and discussed above are consistent with what we might
expect from the operation of precisely such a strategy. So at least are

the signs of some of the smaller correlations, especially those suggesting that neighborhoods in Elyria with higher proportions of blacks receive less aggressive and more watchmanlike policing than do others with smaller black populations.

To a certain extent, styles of policing vary across the neighborhoods of Elyria in ways that are patterned and systematic. To be sure, the city's central business district is a functionally and socially unique area, requiring and receiving a relatively unique style of police service. In residential neighborhoods, however, the character of the local environment does not seem to operate in any simple and direct way to dictate police strategy. Rather, it seems more accurate to say that neighborhood character interacts with organizational operating style; in attempting to maintain the support of its major constituents and its own freedom of action, the police organization structures its patterns of service to simultaneously avoid trouble in one part of town while demonstrating satisfactory levels of "effective" performance in another.

Columbia

In turning to Columbia, we encounter a problem similar to that with which we introduced our ecological analysis of Elyria: too few neighborhood areas—in this instance, 13—to facilitate a detailed examination of spatial distributions of social characteristics across the city's geography. Again, we can look reasonably only to summary statistics and general clustering patterns for the measures of neighborhood character of interest here. Table 6.4 displays the former, which on the whole reaffirm the impression that emerged from the narrative descriptions offered in chapter 3; in terms of the basic background characteristics of their respective populations, Columbia and Elyria are quite different places. The "typical" neighborhood area of the former, compared to that of the latter, is slightly poorer and has a substantially larger black minority. Its population is more residentially mobile, less dominated by married adults and homeowners, and notably more professional in terms of the occupations of its members. In many ways, these differences are not surprising, for Columbia—as governmental hub, educational center, and army base—is sufficiently diverse as a functional entity to attract, house, and maintain a sizable

Table 6.4. The Character of Columbia's Neighborhoods

Variables	Descriptive Statistics	
(N = 13)	Means	Standard Deviations
Percent Black	29.0	30.9
Percent Children	7.1	1.7
Median Income	$8,088	$3,377
Percent Elderly	9.5	3.3
Percent Teenagers	12.5	5.8
Percent Married	54.3	13.2
Percent Foreign-Born	0.9	0.7
Median Years of Schooling	11.8	2.0
Percent Residentially Immobile	52.5	10.3
Percent Professionals	18.5	8.6
Percent Working Women	42.3	4.8
Household Density	2.9	0.4
Median Value of Homes	$17,226	$4,837
Percent Owner-Occupancy	47.4	23.9

population that is in many ways nontraditional for an urban area. This diversity of population is further underscored by the fact, clarified by a quick comparison of tables 6.4 and 6.1, that the characteristics which most clearly distinguish Columbia from Elyria at the neighborhood level of analysis—specifically, the percentages of blacks, teenagers, married adults, professionals, and owner-occupied housing units—are also those on which Columbia's neighborhoods are, as a group, more varied than Elyria's.

While neighborhood diversity is a rather obvious characteristic of Columbia, and while neighborhoods in it differ in many ways from those that compose Elyria, the two cities share some ecological patterns, and to a degree that cannot be dismissed as trivial. Table 6.5, which displays the results of a principal components factor analysis of the 14 area-level characteristics applied to Columbia's 13 neighborhoods, makes that relatively clear. The table presents factor loadings and communality indices for all 14 social and demographic measures, as did the earlier table 6.1 for the results of the Elyria factor analysis. In Columbia, neighborhoods can apparently be distinguished from each other on the basis of each of four dimensions of differentiation. The first of these can readily be labeled "socioeconomic status,"

Table 6.5. Factor Loadings and Communalities in
Columbia

Variables:	Factor Loadings				Communality
	1	2	3	4	
Blacks	−.666	−.255	.157	−.567	.855
Children	−.513	.510	.525	−.154	.823
Income	.915	.355	.058	.127	.982
Elderly	−.098	.352	−.843	.003	.844
Teenagers	−.111	−.979	.148	−.035	.994
Married	.386	.899	.148	.114	.992
Foreign-Born	.195	−.049	−.190	.685	.547
Schooling	.889	−.008	.013	.402	.952
Residential Immobility	.132	.737	−.055	−.210	.607
Professionals	.903	−.046	−.207	.187	.896
Working Women	−.209	.816	−.041	.087	.719
Density	−.123	.147	.883	−.304	.909
Home Values	.936	.014	.021	−.082	.884
Owner-Occupancy	.607	.600	.379	.301	.964
% of Variance Explained	41.2	26.7	15.7	7.2	

combining at its high polar position high home values and income and educational levels, high proportions of professionals, relatively high proportions of owner-occupied homes, and low proportions of blacks. As a glance back at table 6.2 will reveal, this is virtually a carbon copy of what emerged for Elyria's neighborhoods.

Stage in the family life-cycle in Columbia is not so easily defined and labeled ecologically as it was in Elyria; in the former, in fact, this general indicator is divisible into two separate factorial components. The first of those might be labeled a "household character" dimension, linking at its high polar position relatively few teenagers and relatively many working women, married couples, and residentially immobile families. Note here that, as in Elyria, in Columbia contemporary familism involves more rather than fewer working female spouses. The second component of familism seems a matter of "population age structure," linking high levels of household density and high proportions of children to low percentages of the elderly. Finally, Columbia offers a fourth residual differentiating dimension, focused on the relative dominance of the foreign-born in local neighborhood populations. On balance, the ecological structure of Columbia's neighborhoods would appear to be a bit more elaborate than was the case in Elyria. The elaboration involved here, however, is best characterized as a matter of difference in degree rather than in kind. What differentiates neighborhoods in Elyria is the same basic set of dynamics that differentiates them in Columbia.

With regard to the dimensions of police style that they experience, as with regard to the basic background characteristics of their resident populations, Columbia's neighborhood's are a varied lot. On the average, the city's 13 local neighborhoods experience 91.5 nontraffic, police-initiated calls per thousand population per year while, on the average, 46.7 percent of an area's police events are watchmanlike. In both cases, however, these means mask a great deal of variation in actual scores, albeit more so for aggressiveness, which varies from a low value of 9.9 to a high value of 214.2 calls per thousand people per year than for watchman percentages, which vary absolutely between 32.9 and 58.8 percent.

In Elyria, policing the central business district is something of a unique type of work, more aggressive and less watchmanlike than in any other residential neighborhood. Nonetheless, in the neighborhoods of Elyria, police aggressiveness and a watchmanlike workload are highly correlated, with more of the one associated with less of the other, and this whether the central business district is included in or excluded from the analysis. In Columbia, things are somewhat different. The central business district is, indeed, the area of greatest police aggressiveness of all of Columbia's neighborhoods; at the same time, it is a very average place in terms of its proportion of watchmanlike calls, which stands at 47.0 percent. (The neighborhood-level mean percentage is 46.7.) Partly as a result of this, aggressiveness and watchmanism in police work are not that strongly correlated in Columbia. Across all 13 of the city's neighborhoods, the relevant coefficient is a mere $r = -.166$; excluding the central business district from the calculation inflates this figure only marginally, to $r = -.217$. More watchmanlike residential neighborhoods in Columbia do see less aggressive levels of police work, but the degree to which this generalization holds is a good deal lower than it was in Elyria.

Table 6.6 displays the ecological correlates of police aggressiveness and the watchmanlike police workload in Columbia, and does so in the same style of presentation used in table 6.3 for Elyria. Independent variables are grouped by their loadings on the city's larger ecological dimensions and, within groupings, by the strength of their factor loadings. The left-hand columns of coefficients are based on all 13 of Columbia's neighborhoods; the right-hand columns use as cases only the 12 more residential areas. Of course, since the central business district was relatively average on its proportion of watchmanlike calls, the differences in correlations before and after its exclusion should be, and in fact are, quite marginal.

In some ways, the ecological correlates of the two dimensions of local police style in Columbia resemble rather strongly the counter-

Table 6.6. Ecological Correlates of Police Work in Columbia

Neighborhood Measures	All Areas (N = 13)		Residential Areas (N = 12)	
	Police Aggressiveness	Relative Watchmanism	Police Aggressiveness	Relative Watchmanism
I. Socioeconomic Status				
Home Values	-.025	-.290	.107	-.293
Income	-.048	-.174	.197	-.179
Professionals	.006	-.220	.195	-.224
Schooling	-.028	-.243	.316	-.263
Blacks	-.195	.193	-.508	.199
Owner-Occupancy	-.134	-.262	.181	-.285
II. Household Character				
Teenagers	.301	.023	.086	.019
Married	-.183	-.161	.063	-.169
Working Women	-.401	.181	-.131	.221
Residential Immobility	.064	-.168	.068	-.168
III. Age Structure				
Density	-.164	-.299	-.161	-.299
Elderly	.071	.130	.121	.131
Children	-.472	-.087	-.417	-.087
IV. Foreign-Born				
Foreign-Born	-.226	.097	-.022	.109

part findings that emerged in Elyria. One of the most notable of those resemblances is in the quite modest magnitude of those correlations, taken together as a set. Further, there is no consistent pattern of findings to emerge across or within the groupings of independent variables presented in table 6.6. Focusing on individual variables does not improve matters, for only three of the 28 coefficients depicted in the right-hand panels of the table attain magnitudes greater than .3 or less than − .3. On that basis alone, it seems quite clear that environmental variations in general do not structure styles of police action in the predominantly residential neighborhoods in Columbia. As in Elyria, strategies of police style determination in Columbia are based on more specific environmental contingencies.

This latter point can be further specified, for if the findings in table 6.6 say anything in general about residential policing in Columbia, it is that socioeconomic status is the environmental variation that "matters," for the various family measures with one exception show only negligible correlations[4] with the dimensions of police action; to an admittedly modest degree, areas containing high status populations receive relatively more aggressive and less watchmanlike police service than do their lower-status counterparts; and black areas receive slightly more watchmanlike and notably less aggressive styles of policing than do their white counterparts.

The second of these patterns is relatively similar to what emerged in Elyria. In terms of general directions of effects, so for that matter is the third; the difference is a matter of degree, which is marginal in Elyria and more notable in Columbia. With the exception of the race-aggressiveness association, however, these are only relatively modest tendencies in the findings for policing in Columbia.

Conflict theory as a vehicle for interpreting the link between neighborhood character and the style of local police action fares no better in this analysis of Columbia than it did in the preceding treatment of Elyria. If anything, it fares worse. The fact that neighborhoods with sizable black populations receive marginally less legalistic and markedly less aggressive policing in Columbia, where blacks are in fact more numerous than they are in Elyria, only magnifies the difficulty of applying hypotheses derived from conflict theory to the study of police styles. At the same time, however, it further reinforces the strength of a more organizational interpretation of these findings. Consider again a police organization as a corporate actor pursuing a survival strategy and public support in a differentiated urban environment. The strategy it pursues is and should be a bit different in a more legalistic police department like Columbia's from what it is in a more watchmanlike agency like Elyria's. In a legalistic agency, police initiation of encounters with citizens is encouraged and rewarded; as a result, the possibility of conflict inherent in such encounters is magnified. Such an agency need not take special steps to underline its visibility in the community generally or among the resourceful specifically; it virtually accomplishes that "by definition" in the choice and execution of the overall legalistic style. The concern that does require special attention is that of enhanced possibilities for serious conflict with sizable minority communities of the resourceless. These communities the legalistic agency must treat with "kid gloves," especially if they contain sizable blocs of the city's citizens and are capable of mounting a political response to police policy and performance. The sizable negative correlation between police aggressiveness and the percentage of blacks in a neighborhood's population, and the sizable proportion of blacks in Columbia's total population, suggest precisely such a strategy.

In the comparisons of police aggressiveness and substantive legalism offered in chapter 5, Elyria and Columbia emerged—both as complete cities and as collections of diverse internal areas—as relatively dissimilar places. With regard to substantive legalism, the two were not simply different but were, in fact, almost polar opposites. From what has been presented here, there is now evidence to suggest that in neither Elyria nor Columbia is the predominant police style primarily a function of the attempt to control the resourceless; in both, rather, the environmental basis of neighborhood policing, to the relatively modest extent that one emerges, seems rooted in the functional prerequisites for police organizational survival and avoidance of threat. Each of these cases, in its own way, suggests that a simple stimulus → response model where environmental character defines the former and police style the latter is, in fact, too simple if not downright misleading. What rather emerges is a picture of two police organizations pursuing different missions in their respective service domains, with each structuring the way it provides its services to the segments of those domains in such a way as to maintain its freedom of action in pursuit of its overall mission.

Newark

Newark is distinguished among the cities of central interest in this study not only for being the largest and for having the largest police department, but also for having a relatively unique collection of neighborhoods when compared with those in Elyria and Columbia. The descriptive statistics on the social and economic characteristics of Newark's neighborhoods are displayed in table 6.7, and a brief comparison of them with the figures in tables 6.1 and 6.4 will bear out the assertion about uniqueness. The "typical" Newark neighborhood is composed of notably higher proportions of blacks and the foreign-born, of homes with notably lower economic values and, most tellingly of all, of far lower proportions of owner-occupied residences than are our two other cities. Its people are a good deal poorer than are those in Elyria's typical neighborhood, and somewhat poorer than are those in Columbia's; proportionately fewer of the people in a Newark neigh-

Table 6.7. The Character of Newark's Neighborhoods

Variables (N = 25)	Descriptive Statistics	
	Means	Standard Deviations
Percent Black	58.6	34.4
Percent Children	10.7	2.3
Median Income	$7,405	$1,710
Percent Elderly	8.3	4.8
Percent Teenagers	8.6	1.2
Percent Married	56.3	3.8
Percent Foreign-Born	10.0	11.9
Median Years of Schooling	10.0	1.1
Percent Residentially Immobile	48.1	10.1
Percent Professionals	7.7	4.8
Percent Working Women	40.0	7.7
Household Density	3.1	0.4
Median Value of Homes	$14,900	$2,883
Percent Owner-Occupancy	17.6	8.6

borhood are likely to be married than is the case in Elyria, and proportionately fewer Newark neighborhood residents are working in
professional or technical jobs than their counterparts in Columbia.
Compared with Elyria and Columbia, then, Newark is a city of poor,
renter neighborhoods in which minority ethnic groups tend in fact to
constitute the proportional majority.

In this same comparative perspective, the overall urban ecology at
Newark is just as unique as are many of its specific neighborhood-level
characteristics. Table 6.8 demonstrates this rather clearly, in the form
of factor loadings and communality indices from a principal components, orthogonal-rotation factor analysis applied to 13 of the fourteen
neighborhood measures and all 25 of Newark's internal neighborhoods. The median home value measure is the one excluded from this
procedure. This slight deviation from past practice in conducting factor analyses is dictated by the fact that so few homes are owned in
Newark by those residing in them that the measure captures something characteristic of only the smallest portion of the neighborhood
for which it is calculated. In more than one Newark census tract and,
as a result, in one of the neighborhoods constructed for this study by

Table 6.8. Factor Loadings and Communalities in
Newark

Variables	Factor Loadings			Communality
	1	2	3	
Blacks	.701	−.430	.430	.861
Children	.720	−.434	.172	.736
Income	−.382	.912	.141	.998
Elderly	−.817	.032	−.238	.725
Teenagers	.782	−.137	−.377	.773
Married	.120	.790	−.215	.685
Foreign-Born	−.434	.561	−.556	.812
Schooling	−.160	.292	.876	.879
Residential Immobility	−.126	.070	−.659	.454
Professionals	−.621	.187	.664	.862
Working Women	−.031	.788	.382	.767
Density	.913	.102	−.211	.889
Owner-Occupancy	−.169	.840	.091	.743
% of Variance Explained	42.0	21.7	18.9	

aggregating tracts and police beats, so few homes are owned that the census reports no figures whatsoever on median home values. Rather than losing one of a relatively small number of cases, and because other neighborhood-level measures of socioeconomic status are available, we have excluded that measure from the factor analysis.

As table 6.8 demonstrates, Newark's neighborhoods are effectively differentiated from each other by three general ecological dimensions. The first dimensions clusters a set of population measures, linking at its highest level high proportions of blacks, children, and teenagers and high levels of household density with low proportions of the elderly. Note that this is the first city-level analysis in which race has not been directly linked with low socioeconomic status. The other two differentiators appear to be two different types of socioeconomic status or, perhaps more accurately, reflections of two different pathways to status attainment. The first (factor 2) is a more local path, the second (factor 3) a more cosmopolitan one. Local status clusters high levels of income, marriage, employment for women, and owner-occupancy with high proportions of the foreign-born and, in so doing, reflects a "bootstraps" strategy of success to be attained by earning an income and owning a home. Cosmopolitan status links high levels of schooling and professional employment with low levels of residential stability; effectively, it reflects a "credentials" strategy of success to be attained by being a mobile, educated professional. In some ways, these empirical results suggest that Newark on a more local scale distributes its people across ecological space in accordance with their positions in the larger, national dual economy (Hodson and Kaufman 1982).

Police work in Newark as a whole and across its specific neighborhoods is more aggressive than it is in either Elyria or Columbia, but it is relatively middle-range in terms of substantive style; less watchmanlike than Elyria, but less legalistic than Columbia. As a result, Newark is relatively middle-range with regard to the degree to which police work there is a neat empirical combination of those two dimensions. Aggressiveness rates across its 25 neighborhoods average 156.1 police-initiated nontraffic events per thousand residents per year, with specific neighborhoods' scores varying wildly between a low of 51.4 and a high of 756.6. Similarly, proportions of watchmanlike calls average 68.7 percent in a "typical" neighborhood, with actual figures varying between a low of 57 and a high of 77 percent. Across all 25 neighborhoods, police aggressiveness and watchmanlike work are correlated strongly at $r = -.663$. All of these figures, however, are affected by the extremes of downtown policing for, as in Elyria and in Columbia, the three neighborhoods in Newark that include the central business district experience extremely aggressive police work (with rates of 756.6, 452.1, and 398.9 police-initiated calls per thousand residents per year) and relatively less watchmanlike mixes of calls (with the relevant percentages falling at 57, 60, and 60). Excluding these three areas from the analysis shrinks the correlation between aggressiveness and watchmanism to a more modest $r = -.476$ in Newark, which in turn is almost exactly half the difference between the much weaker figure comparable for Columbia ($r = -.217$) and the much stronger one for Elyria ($r = -.709$).

The environmental bases for neighborhood-level police aggressiveness and watchmanlike work in Newark, such as they are, are depicted in table 6.9. The table displays the relevant correlation coefficients in the same ordering format as used in the comparable earlier tables for Elyria and Columbia. Newark is more like the former than the latter in that excluding the downtown areas makes a notable difference in the ecological correlations for both aspects of police service. It is unlike both, however, with regard to the message carried by those correlation coefficients.

From table 6.9, it is relatively clear that the degree to which a Newark neighborhood is a watchmanlike police area is virtually impervious to environmental variation on virtually every measure studied here. Only one of the 13 coefficients in the far right-hand column of the table—that for residential stability, or immobility—approaches a respectable magnitude, a fact that might have been anticipated from pure chance alone. As we have already seen, the neighborhoods of Newark do not vary capriciously with regard to substantive police style; to the contrary, they cluster around each other and their own particular position on the overall style continuum, just as do the neighborhoods of Elyria or Columbia. We can only conclude from these correlations that in Newark the decision to adopt a particular substantive style is one that is relatively unconstrained—some might say uninformed—by the characteristics of the neighborhoods where that style will be enacted.

Table 6.9. Ecological Correlates of Police Work in Newark

Neighborhood Measures	All Areas (N = 25)		Residential Areas (N = 22)	
	Police Aggres- siveness	Relative Watch- manism	Police Aggres- siveness	Relative Watch- manism
I. Family/Population Structure				
Density	-.574	.303	-.128	.041
Elderly	.190	-.131	.302	-.142
Teenagers	-.495	.152	.163	-.169
Children	-.235	.140	-.075	.003
Blacks	-.105	.148	.082	-.024
II. Socioeconomic Status — Local				
Income	-.012	-.062	-.334	.035
Owner-Occupancy	-.265	.132	-.335	.190
Married	-.421	.207	-.638	.251
Working Women	.192	-.200	-.361	-.035
Foreign-Born	.216	-.288	-.078	-.015
III. Socioeconomic Status — Cosmopolitan				
Schooling	-.001	.075	-.411	.034
Professionals	.309	-.039	-.162	.109
Stability	-.228	-.134	.132	-.355
(Home Values, N = 24,21)	-.223	.247	-.335	.190

Such is patently not the case, however, with regard to police aggressiveness. For this dimension of police style in Newark, the environment counts for quite a lot, and it does so in a way that is not found in either Elyria or Columbia. Newark offers the first set of correlations to emerge from this study that are consistent with the expectations derived from conflict theory. Population structure predicts nothing in a consistent way about aggressiveness; cosmopolitan economic status fares little better. Local economic status differentiations, however, are key; the lower the local socioeconomic status of an area, the more aggressive the police work it experiences. The correlation coefficients linking all five of the specific elements of this general ecological dimension to police aggressiveness are consistently negative, and four of the five are of sufficient magnitude to be worthy of comment. In general, then, the more resourceless an area in Newark, the more its police inject themselves into the flow of its local social life.

These findings from Newark, when juxtaposed with those from Elyria and Columbia, pose a rather striking anomaly: why should a hypothesis derived from conflict theory be rather strikingly confirmed in one city, and yet rather tellingly disconfirmed in the other two? Is there a simple size ratchet at work here, such that larger cities generate higher levels of disorder than smaller ones, and thus require the exercise of more proactive social control by the forces of the state? A formal evaluation of that proposition is not possible with the data at hand from this study, but the argument is certainly consistent with the position taken by the classical urban sociologists. Louis Wirth, perhaps the most prominent of them, argued (1938) that the city—specifically the large, dense heterogeneous city—is a destroyer of the simple premodern moral order, based as it is in primordial ties generated from family, kin, ethnic, and class distinctions. In Wirth's model,[5] urbanization gives rise to institutional differentiation and, with it, institutional formality in dealing with an increasingly disordered world. A Wirthian perspective would attempt to explain the empirical anomaly uncovered here by focusing on the size, density, and heterogeneity of Newark relative to Elyria and Columbia, arguing that these generate a more disorderly world while simultaneously vesting the task of controlling it in the hands of formal and institutionally specialized forces of order, chief among them the police.

Wirth's argument has been attacked by scholars as being exceedingly and unrealistically mechanistic (Fischer 1981; Smith 1979); in some ways, it has been at least partially disconfirmed by empirical research. Its application to these findings on police aggressiveness from Elyria, Columbia, and Newark—and specifically to the anomaly they pose—provides an explanation for them only if we paper over both the relative similarity of Newark and Columbia in police aggressiveness rates (and the corresponding dissimilarity of Columbia and Elyria in this regard) and the general lack of correspondence between rankings of these three cities on size, or more generally on urbanization, on the one hand and on the substantive styles of police work they experience on the other. That seems an inordinately heavy price to pay to make a theory work; in fact, it cannot help but cast doubt on the basic validity and utility of any theory that would demand such a sacrifice of empirical findings.

An organizational perspective on police styles can account for this anomaly, which proves so elusive for classical theories of urbanization. As was noted in chapter 5, the findings on levels of police aggressiveness in Elyria, Columbia, and Newark are consistent with Michael Brown's hypothesis that the larger the police agency, and the broader its typical supervisory span of control, the greater the opportunity for the exercise of discretion by its individual members, especially those on the patrol force. The key question, in light of that hypothesis, becomes: discretion for what? It is here that the matter of organizational style comes to the fore. The police department that adopts a relatively "pure" style—be it the relative watchmanism of Elyria or the relative legalism of Columbia—imposes on itself the problem of justification to its public, which is generally rather well aware that police work is a congeries of very different functions, duties, and services. By the same token, the agency that adopts a more mixed style—like Newark in this study—is, by definition, doing a little bit of everything in nearly every neighborhood it serves. It need not justify itself to anywhere near the same degree.

This problem of justification poses the constraints on discretion that dictate its exercise in differing service environments. In a predominantly watchmanlike police agency, the problem of justification is one of "showing the flag," demonstrating that its members are in fact present and vigilant even if their work is generally reactive and often unnoticed. In a predominantly legalistic agency, the problem of justification is one of "knowing limits," demonstrating that its proactive, law-enforcing members are not so aggressive or insensitive as to provoke unnecessary confrontations and serious disorders, especially vis-à-vis the members of minority groups. In the mixed-style agency, there is no concomitant problem of justification. Its members are relatively free to get on with the business of what they see as "real" police work: making arrests, conducting investigations, and resolving disorders.

The heart of this argument comes down to a focus on three variables: the size of the police department, the width of its typical street-level supervisory span of control, and the style or mission that it defines for itself. The first two typically occur together, and typically offer police officers more opportunities for the exercise of discretion, while the last directs that exercise in the service of organizational ends. Newark's police department combines large size and a relatively broad span of control with a mixed police style to offer its officers discretion to be used to control the resourceless. In Elyria and Columbia, smaller agencies with concomitantly narrower spans of control and with purer police styles offer their members less discretion and focus even that on resolving the problem of justifying their efforts to the resourceful in their respective communities. As we saw in chapter 3, police department sizes in Ohio, South Carolina, and New Jersey are predominantly functions of the sizes of the cities they serve, but departmental styles are not so mechanistically determined by the environment. There is evidence that the choice of a particular substantive police style is structured by the command system extant in the police agency and the connections between it and local political/administrative structures in the city. This in itself, however, suggests a complicated linkage between environment and style that is, in effect, mediated by the organization. One needs to take seriously the police organization as an actor, pursuing working strategies toward organizational ends, before one can really understand what James Q. Wilson called the "varieties of police behavior."

Style and Neighborhood Effects: An Intercity Comparison

The case for the superiority of an organizational over an environmental perspective for interpreting and understanding urban police styles seems, from the findings presented in this chapter, rather clear and compelling. Nevertheless, that case can be further reinforced or, alternatively, substantially undercut by one last, more rigorous test that compares the dimensions of police style simultaneously across the 50 neighborhoods of Elyria, Columbia, and Newark, taken together. That test uses two associated statistical procedures, analysis of variance and multiple classification analysis. The dependent variables for both will be the same two dimensions of police style of interest throughout this chapter: the rate of local police aggressiveness, and the substantive watchmanlike weight in the local police workload. Note that across all 50 neighborhoods, the two are relatively distinct aspects of policing, with the simple correlation between them amounting to only a modest $r = -.242$, in turn shrinking only marginally to $r = -.204$ across the 45 primarily residential neighborhoods of the three cities. Independent variables for the intercity analyses of these two dimensions of police style will be (a) the city in which a neighborhood is located, (b) whether or not a neighborhood is part of its city's central business district, and (c) selected measures from those reported above of the social and economic characteristics of each of the 50 neighborhoods.

In a sense, this test seems something of an anticlimax. In fact, it is a good deal more than that, at least on a theoretical plane. But for the effects attributable to downtown policing, most of the city-level differences in the dimensions of police style identified across our three cities have been associated with and attributed to concomitant differences in the structures of their police organizations and the strategic choices of missions made by those agencies. The results of the city-level ecological analyses undertaken in this chapter have done little to alter that style of analysis or the interpretations drawn from it. Nonetheless, separate city-level analyses can mask systematic, across-city effects. Suppose, for the sake of argument, that some identifiable aspect of the urban environment among those used in the prior analysis was differentially distributed across our cities so that neighborhoods in one city scored uniformly high on that variable, neighborhoods in the second scored uniformly low, while neighborhoods in the third consistently fell in the middle range of scores. City-specific studies correlating the elements of police style with this hypothetical variable would necessarily work within a truncated range of variation on the latter. They could well produce correlations varying in sign and magnitude primarily because of this truncated variance problem, while across the full range of variation in the environmental characteristic a more systematic effect might be at work. Such an effect, were it to emerge, would certainly be environmental or situational, and would go a long way toward resurrecting the argument for style determination based on such factors.[6]

Table 6.10 reports correlational results for the ecological analysis of the two dimensions of police style, calculated across all 50 neighborhoods. Like its counterpart tables for the city-specific analyses, table 6.10 reports correlational results separately for (a) all 50 neighborhoods and (b) the 45 more residential or non-business-district areas in the three cities. The right-hand panel of table 6.10 is the one on which to focus. For a measure of local environmental character to have a notable effect on either dimension of police style in this en-

Table 6.10. Ecological Correlates of Police Action Across All
Three Cities

	All Areas (N = 50)		Residential Areas (N = 45)	
Environmental Characteristics	Police Aggressiveness	Relative Watchmanism	Police Aggressiveness	Relative Watchmanism
Income	-.211	.106	-.348**	.065
Schooling	-.211	-.228	-.274**	-.321**
Professionals	-.010	-.448**	-.100	-.494**
Home Values*	-.199	-.132	-.173	-.182
Owner-Occupancy	-.401**	-.076	-.415**	-.147
Married	-.312**	.283**	.363**	.225
Working Women	.098	-.201	-.242	-.243
Residential Immobility	-.197	-.141	.028	-.171
Density	-.404**	.328**	-.145	.310**
Children	-.096	.485**	-.064	.461**
Elderly	.121	-.074	.169	-.062
Teenagers	-.106	-.377**	.053	-.370**
Blacks	.146	.096	.252**	.109
Foreign-Born	.316**	.115	.113	.216

* N's = 49,44, respectively.
** Significant at $p \leq .05$.

larged comparative analysis, given the previously identified importance of city and business district status in this regard, it will have to
correlate strongly with one or both of the police style measures across
all of the residential neighborhood areas. Picking for the analysis of
variance environmental measures that meet this standard is, in effect,
to "stack the deck" as much as possible in that analysis in favor of the
environmental argument for the determination of police style.

From table 6.10, it seems rather clear that the strongest candidate
measures for inclusion in the analyses of variance among all the environmental variables listed are: median income, median schooling,
percent of professionals, percent of adults who are married, percent
owner-occupied housing, average household density, percent children,
percent teenagers, and percent black. The first, second, fourth, fifth,
and last correlate at statistically significant levels with police aggressiveness; the second, third, sixth, seventh and eighth do likewise
with the measure of substantive police watchmanism. Across all 45 of

our residential neighborhoods, the areas that experience more aggressive police work tend to hold more blacks, fewer married adults and, in general, fewer resource-rich persons. Similarly, areas that receive more watchmanlike policing tend to have more young children and fewer teenagers among their residents, and tend also to contain fewer educated professionals. On the whole, these results for police aggressiveness are more reminiscent of the findings for Newark than for either Columbia or Elyria while, on the whole, the results for substantive watchmanism seem more reminiscent of the Columbia analysis.

In table 6.11 are presented the results of the analyses of variance and the multiple classification analyses.[7] The structure of the table is relatively straightforward. Its two panels present separate sets of analytic results for each of the two dependent variables. In the first row of each panel are displayed the effects (in the form of Beta coefficients) of city and central business district status on police action as uncovered by the multiple classification analyses, and the results of significance tests for those effects as produced by the concomitant two-way analyses of variance. In subsequent rows, the same effects are displayed for the same two independent variables and for each of the environmental measures introduced when the analytic routine is expanded to a three-way treatment. The far right-hand column of table 6.11 presents values of R^2, the proportion of variance in the police action measure accounted for by the two or three independent variables included in the different analyses. Results for three-way analyses based on the inclusion of the income and schooling measures, where police aggressiveness is the dependent variable, are not depicted in the table, because median income, median schooling, percent professionals, and percent of owner-occupancy are all heavily intercorrelated (with values of Pearson's r ranging between .703 and .861), making some of them virtually redundant. The former two can be safely eliminated in favor of the two stronger correlates of police aggressiveness for purposes of this comparative test.

We need not belabor the results contained in table 6.11, for as it happens, they really are relatively anticlimactic. Between them, the city in which a neighborhood is located and the status of that neighborhood—residential or business—explain nearly two-thirds and three-quarters of the variance in police aggressiveness and substantive

Table 6.11. City, Business-District and Environmental Effects
on Police Action

Environmental Measure Introduced	City	Values of B Associated with Business District Status	Environmental Charactersitic	R^2
I. Police Aggressiveness				
None	.35*	.71*	—	.655
Owner-Occupancy	.47*	.72*	.24**	.697
Blacks	.37*	.72*	.06	.659
Married	.45*	.67*	.20	.685
II. Relative Watchmanism				
None	.86*	.24*	—	.786
Professionals	.87*	.23*	.05	.787
Children	.87*	.24*	.04	.788
Teenagers	.87*	.24*	.03	.787

* Analysis of variance produced an F-statistic in the test for statistical significance sufficiently strong such that the associated F-probability fell at or below $p = .05$.

** Effect statistically significant at $p = .058$.

police watchmanism, respectively, with each predictor making a separate significant causal contribution to each dependent variable. Intercity differences are particularly strong for substantive police watchmanism; the business/residential status of the neighborhood is the primary predictor of police aggressiveness. In no instance does the addition of a third environmental variable significantly alter these results. None of the included environmental measures increment R^2 by more than .042; none make what little contribution they do at the expense of either city or business-district status, but rather in addition; put simply, none add much that is unique about police aggressiveness or the watchmanlike police style, relative to what was uncovered about both in the prior analyses. In those few instances where a measure of neighborhood character makes something more than a negligible contribution to the analysis, that contribution appears to be curvilinear. Neighborhoods in the high and low categories on both the proportion of teenagers and the percent of owner-occupied homes receive less aggressive, more watchmanlike police service; those in the medium category on each independent variable see the reverse. If anything, such patterns would suggest that, for both variables in question, it is not the extreme situation that elicits agressive, legalistic policing but rather the more ambigious, middle-ground one, in which labeling of a neighborhood and its character and knowing how to respond to that label seem much more difficult for both police and public alike. Even so, however, these effects of the presence of teenagers' and owner-occupancy rates are clearly "also rans" in light of the weights attached by the analyses summarized in table 6.11 to city and to business-district status as determinants of the style of local policing.

The importance of police strategy choices, organizational structures, and internal police agency dynamics in the patterning of local police work have not been undercut, nor even seriously challenged, in this intercity analysis. To be sure, police departments face a common functional problem in policing the central business districts of their cities, a problem to which they respond in common ways: more police aggressiveness and less watchmanlike policing. Beyond that, however, the environment is simply a stage, and police organizations the actors. They choose missions, design strategies to fulfill them, and execute those strategies on the local stage. The character of the neighborhood in which police work is carried out does not serve in any mechanistic causal way to produce one or another kind of police service. If anything, it serves as a congeries of constraints to police organizations; to fulfill their missions, they may have to tailor their service strategies a bit in response to those local constraints. As we have seen, however, the degree of tailoring required is fairly minimal. There is relatively little of situational determinism here, but relatively much of pragmatic, rational, organizationally chosen action.

Notes

1. Specifically, these ranges amounted to 28.8 percentage points in Elyria, 25.9 points in Columbia and 19.2 points in Newark. Across all the neighborhoods regardless of their city locations, the range on watchmanlike proportions amounted to 54.7 percentage points.
2. Variables 11 and 13 would be negative indicators; variables 12 and 14, positive ones.

3. Factor analysis is essentially a statistical technique for data reduction that searches a matrix of correlation coefficients for a smaller number of underlying dimensions or factors that can account for patterns in that matrix. A full technical discussion of the method is available in Harman (1976); an eminently readable account for those less mathematically oriented is offered in Gould (1981), along with a discussion of its uses and abuses in a specific research context.

4. Even the exception, the percentage of children present in an area, is itself heavily correlated with educational attainments $(r = -.491)$ and the percentage of professionals in the local populations $(r = -.629)$. Given this, it is difficult to attribute any serious importance to this measure.

5. Fischer (1972) provides a systematization of Wirth's original argument that makes this abundantly clear.

6. To illustrate that this is not a completely hypothetical argument, note that percent of owner-occupied homes and police aggressiveness (as environmental and police variables, respectively) work in a fashion similar to that outlined hypothetically here. Owner-occupancy is highest in Elyria, while police aggressiveness is lowest; occupancy and aggressiveness take on middle-range values in Columbia; owner-occupancy is lowest and police aggressiveness highest in Newark. Note further that occupancy and aggressive police action are positively correlated in Elyria $(r = .298)$, virtually independent in Columbia $(r = .181)$ and negatively correlated in Newark $(r = -.335)$. It is precisely because of a pattern like this and its implications for the argument on organization developed earlier that our across-city analysis takes on such importance.

7. Analysis of variance requires that the independent variables with which it works all be categorical. We can most easily and reliably change the environmental measures from the ratio level of measurement to the ordinal by

Table 6.12. Effects of Trichotomization on Environment-Police Correlates

	Police Aggressiveness		*Relative Watchmanism*	
		Pearson's		*Pearson's*
Environmental Variables:	*Eta[7]*	*r*	*Eta*	*r*
Professionals	—	—	.21	− .45
Children	—	—	.47	.49
Teenagers	—	—	.33	− .38
Density	—	—	.33	.33
Owner-Occupancy	.48	− .40	—	—
Blacks	.28	.15	—	—
Married	.33	− .31	—	—

trichotomizing their distributions into nearly equally populated categories of low, medium, and high, and have done so for this analysis. That procedure, however, raises a question: does the sacrifice of precision in these environmental variables seriously affect their respective associations with the measures of police action? The answer is that it generally does not, as demonstrated in table 6.12. If the environment is to have an effect on police action across the 45 residential neighborhoods studied here, that effect should emerge relatively clearly from the analysis of these trichotomized indicators. Note, with regard to table 6.12, that by virtue of the formula from which it is calculated, eta can never take on a negative value. Thus, while actual values of eta and r are displayed, the appropriate comparison is between an eta and the absolute value of the corresponding Pearson's r.

7. Looking Back and Looking Forward

In building their theories about cities and urban life, most of the classical urban sociologists began their theoretical excursions with the three characteristics they thought basic to the definition and the character of the city: its large size, its relatively high level of population density, and its broad population diversity. In America, many places "qualify" as cities when compared with these benchmark variables, but the premiere instance of their combination is, as it has been in the past, New York City. Because of its relative or absolute extremity in terms of these characteristics, New York often offers scholars and commentators pictures of the various phenomena of interest painted in high relief, and that might not emerge so clearly in less complex or highly differentiated settings.

One instance of this is in the area of policing. In any large city that is served by a concomitantly large and functionally complex police department, it is relatively apparent that the interests and attitudes of police executives and their patrol officers will often diverge; in few cities other than New York will those divergences be elaborated into two distinct, competing cultures of policing. That that is true in New York emerges quite clearly from the studies of Elizabeth Reuss-Ianni (1983) and Francis Ianni (Reuss-Ianni and Ianni 1983), who write of the power of street-cop culture, as opposed to the management-cop culture with which it competes, that:

> While either [of the two cultures] may influence the individual [police officer] through his set of values or through his information, our observations convinced us that at this point in time, it is the precinct level or street cop culture values that determine the style and practice of policing. Since these values underwrite and inform the social organization of the precinct, they act as a determinant for behavior and for the dispositions and attitudes of its members. (Reuss-Ianni and Ianni 1983:259)

The phrase "at this point in time" is critical to their discussion, for the authors recognize that adherents of the police management culture monopolize the sources of promotion and prestige within the police hierarchy. Street cops in New York can resist their superiors, and thus maintain the viability of their own culture of policing, "in the only way they have at their disposal: foot-dragging, absenteeism, and a host of similar coping mechanisms and self-defending techniques" (Reuss-Ianni and Ianni, 1983:270). These are, of course, reactive strategies; they surrender the initiative for structuring police work to the carriers of the management culture. They may at present be more or less effective for preserving street-cop culture and for defining the character of local police work, but the power of management to exert its prerogatives would appear to be the odds-on favorite for the future.

In many ways, this book suggests that that future is now. It does not deal with police officers' attitudes and dispositions, nor in any explicit sense with their two cultures. It does deal with the dimensions of police action, however, and it does test whether precinct-level or beat-level social realities determine those dimensions both within and across selected American cities. That those beat-level realities are less salient generators of the dimensions of police style than are police organizational processes and strategies is its major message.

In developing that message, this book has covered much methodological and substantive ground, ground that is worth recapping. That is in part the purpose of this final chapter. In equal part, however, its purpose is to look forward. To view a police organization as a relatively rational corporate actor that devises strategies and seeks out public support is to take a perspective that, while not particularly common in the field, nonetheless opens new or reopens old issues around the role of the police in contemporary urban society. This book would be remiss if it ended with only a simple summary of findings. Accordingly, this concluding chapter moves from a look back at what we have found to a look forward to what we should seek in subsequent studies of police.

In Retrospect

Most contemporary studies of police action seek to uncover the effects of policing on the people it touches; most typically ask whether variations in police activity result in reduced crime or victimization rates, in heightened perceptions among citizens of their personal security and safety, or in more effective control of the sources of urban disorder. Compared to the deterrence or effectiveness studies, relatively few current research efforts attempt to seek out the sources of those variations in police activity; of those that do, most look either to the city as a whole (e.g., Liska and Chamlin 1985) or to the individual police officer (e.g., Brown 1981) as container or as carrier, respectively, of police work. Virtually none look between the two, to the precincts or neighborhoods where police work is conducted, in search of its primary determinants. As a result, virtually none can pose and answer the question of "organization versus environment" in the structuring of the totality of police action and the style characteristic of its conduct.

To answer that question—to take that precinct-level look at police work and to compare what it reveals across other precincts in the same and in other cities—requires data that, unlike arrest and crime rates, are not readily available to researchers. That, in turn, has required that this book be partly "methodological," in the sense that it has had to seek out, develop, and argue for the utility of new kinds of data available for and appropriate to the task at hand. On that basic methodological level, this effort has discovered in the police dispatch log what appears, on balance, to be a solid and worthwhile source of information for empirical research on police activity. Such data are certainly not perfect; the availability of logs from different police departments and the quality of the material collected in them are both variable, the latter apparently more so than the former. That will probably always be the case. The elements of the dispatch log are usually compiled quickly, often in situations of no little anxiety and excitement; once compiled and transmitted by dispatchers to field officers, those data are rarely, if ever, readdressed by field officers, their supervisors, or police executives. There is little reason to believe that the process will change in the near future, given the organization of police work. Yet, these problems of variable availability and quality of data are not insurmountable, and in fact the very same conditions giving rise to them also recommend the use of dispatch data for research. The materials gathered in police dispatch logs generally have a common meaning across the locations where they are collected and therefore can be made comparable for purposes of research. Further, the speed of their collection and the inattention subsequently directed to them combine to enhance their reliability. Unlike reported crime rates—with their marvelous tendency to fall suspiciously in the periods immediately preceding municipal elections (Heinz, Jacob and Lineberry 1983)—or arrest and citation rates—which regularly rise after citizen protests and media-reported crime waves (Fishman 1978)—dispatch log data remain relatively unmanipulated and hence unflawed. Put simply, it is in no one's interest to tamper with them, since no one pays them much attention. For that very reason, they seem attractive materials for use in research.

Among pragmatic scientists, of course, the "proof" of any body of data lies in what it can produce. Here, again, dispatch data have much to recommend them. With specific regard to the concerns that have motivated this study, they make possible the analysis of the most salient dimensions of an important general concept—police style, and they do so in a way: that is related to other similar attempts in the literature but avoids the logical problems they encounter; that is useful at aggregated levels of analysis like the neighborhood or the city as a whole; that reflects the substantive diversity inherent in police work, and thus is realistic; and that yet captures that diversity in an orderly way, highlighting the separable aspects of police style and making each amenable to empirical analysis.

Dispatch data generally offer no simple, single measure of police style; in this particular study, in fact, they yield two analytically and empirically distinct measures of the dimensions of style. Taken together, however, those two indicators tap the most salient aspects of the highly diverse and generally fast-paced world of police work, in the agencies and the geographic areas where that work is actually carried out.

Because they accomplish all this, police dispatch data make possible the testing of a number of substantive hypotheses and the generation of many important empirical findings about the nature of police styles. That, of course, is the real promise that such data offer, and the real story told in this book. We have chosen here to tie this study to one general, overarching question, that of the differential effects of urban environment and police organization on the structuring of street-level police work. This is a critical question for empirical research on the police, one that has been addressed all too infrequently. The answer offered here is consistent with that offered by the relatively few others (Wilson 1972; to some extent Muir 1977; Brown 1981) who have asked it; we and they must point to the critical importance of the organization and, in general, to the relative lack of power of the environment, in generating the major dimensions of police style.

A specification is in order with regard to this general conclusion. It is possible, of course, to define as the environment of a service organization anyone and anything which can be and is touched by that organization and its members. In the context of the police, such a broad definition of the environment would necessarily include the individuals, social groups, and formal organizations residing in the cities they serve; their own friends and members of their own families; media representatives; political elites and influential people to whom they are accountable at the local and state levels of government; professional organizations for police executives and police officers' unions; other law enforcement agencies and personnel; judges and attorneys; probation, parole, and jail officials, and perhaps a host of others as well. Obviously, this is too broad a definition. It subsumes everything under the general label of environment and, by virtue of that, virtually precludes the asking of important, researchable questions.

In this study, we have operated with a much more limited notion of the environment. Those who champion the argument for the situational determination of policing (see, e.g., Manning 1977) usually argue that the moral order of public life is a socially constructed phenomenon, an aggregate of the expectations and interactions of its participants. These will vary from setting to setting with a host of factors,[1] but the moral orders to which those varying factors give rise are nonetheless real. Police officers who would be even minimally effective as agents of formal social control must adapt themselves to and operate within the parameters of these varying moral orders. Where the orders differ within a city, policing will concomitantly differ; where they are similar within or even across cities, policing becomes a more similar task as well. To their credit, situational determinists are generally careful to specify these structured moral orders as the situations or environments with which they are concerned. To speak to that argument, this study has defined the environment of police work as that set of social, economic, demographic, and functional characteristics which differentiate urban subpopulations from each other, and which form the bases for cognitive identifications of and symbolic attachments to the local communities which structure those public moral orders.

The case against the environment as so conceptualized and for the organization as the primary factor in structuring local police styles and patterns emerges from this study in a number of different ways. Using a sample of cities as cases and arrest rates as indicators of legalistic police styles, and playing off against each other as predictors of arrests both city characteristics and police organizational measures, the analyses presented in chapter 2 offered the first hint that the latter were neither theoretically nor empirically trivial. The more finely grained analyses of police work in Elyria, Columbia, and Newark—which used the dispatch log data on police styles and were generally presented in chapters 3 through 6, further elaborated and reenforced this point. Those analyses, to be specific, uncovered these findings:

1. The "style" of local police work—the rate of police aggressiveness and the relative level of watchmanlike police action—is generally similar across the neighborhoods of a given city and generally dissimilar to that in neighborhoods in other cities. The exception to this comes with the central business districts, each of which are indeed environmentally distinct areas that pose locally unique policing problems and that experience locally unique styles of police action. For residential neighborhoods, however, the generalization holds, despite the social, economic, and racial variations that set them off from their counterpart areas in each city studied. This, of course, is the opposite of what is to be expected from the argument for situational determination: stylistic heterogeneity within a city, and homogeneity without.

2. Across the three cities, variations in police style—again, police aggressiveness and watchmanlike levels of local police work—can be statistically accounted for to a high degree, but the variance so explained is attributable to the different cities themselves or to their unique central business districts. Adding to the analysis other specific indicators of environmental characteristics, among them indicators that differentiate the cities from each other rather powerfully, adds virtually nothing to the explanations so generated, and certainly nothing at the expense of the two primary causal agents.

3. Across the three cities, even very general measures of the environmental context fail to say much about variations in local police style. Regional location of a city appears to account for little of the observed variation in police style and, in some ways, produces observations directly contrary to our expectations. Some of the observed variations in police style are probably attributable to variations in city size or, more generally, to a community's

level or degree of urbanization; even here, however, the effect is in all
likelihood an indirect one, operating through the characteristics of the
police departments serving those cities. Finally, the magnitude of the local
crime problem, while it surely figures in the process of police resource
allocation in some cities, seems nonetheless relatively unable to explain
style variations across them.[2]

4. Within the cities studied here, some environmental variations correlate with
police style variations, but the relevant coefficients are generally not very
large. Since the environmental indicators used in this analysis were chosen
for their proven importance as ecological differentiators in American cities,
this relative lack of correlations is indeed notable. In part, this finding may
well be due to the time lapse between the collection of the environmental
indicators and that of the police dispatch data, an interval which is probably
larger than optimal. More notable, however, is the fact that these correlations are not consistent from city to city; in some instances, they yield
precisely opposite results, with the same indicator generating more aggressive and less watchmanlike policing in one city and the reverse in another. These differences, in particular, are too strong to be attributed to
mere statistical artifacts. Moreover, they are particularly damning for the
contention of situational determination of police style.

The case for the importance of the organizational factors in structuring police styles lies in precisely these same points, of course; but it
is more than merely a logical alternative to "what didn't work." Larger
police departments are characterized by broader spans of immediate
supervisory control over police patrol officers and these broader spans
offer patrol officers more opportunities for the exercise of discretion
and the conduct of aggressive police work. In addition, it is also clear
that the organizational command systems generated by varying link-
ages between police and urban officials structure the choice of a
general style, and the constraints of that style focus the discretion
exercised by individual officers and tailor it to the problem of main-
taining organizational freedom of action in a differentiated environment. In this tailoring of street-level police work to better achieve the
larger police agency mission, the organizational perspective can account for most of the differing effects of the same environmental
indicators from city to city. It is, in short, a case that emerges convinc-
ingly in its own right from the research presented throughout this
book.

To state the debate between organization and environment here—
for that matter, in any research context—as a simple choice between

mutually exclusive alternatives is, to be sure, to oversimply the issue. Environments certainly matter to police styles, as this analysis makes abundantly clear. The anomie generated in the central business districts of our cities and the general inability of their relatively few permanent residents to act as informal agents of social control over those districts are countered, in each case, by a police style somewhat more legalistic and strikingly more aggressive than is the case in more residential neighborhoods. Further, police style varies somewhat across the residential neighborhoods of each city as well, as demonstrated by the figures presented in chapter 5, and a small but still nonnegligible proportion of that variance remains unexplained by the statistical analyses presented in chapters 5 and especially 6. Some of this may well be attributable to environmental volatility. Granting this, however, the results compiled in this study point nonetheless to the predominance of the structure and dynamics of the police organization, and not those of the environmental situation, in structuring street-level police work and the style by means of which it is conducted.

In Prospect

While the case for organization seems relatively clear and compelling from the research reported here, there are clearly a good many ways in which subsequent efforts could improve on it. To be sure, methodological refinement through replication is a priority item. The measures of police style on which much of this research are based—the relative proportions of different events in each of the general style categories—would undoubtedly benefit from a more detailed treatment, which would include not simply substantive type and source of initiation but the disposition of the event as well. In this study, data on dispositions unfortunately had to be sacrificed because it was unavailable among the Columbia materials. The disposition of some cases by arrest—especially those involving drunks, vagrants, or other "disorderly" persons—was clearly important in Wilson's original research. While tapping the degree to which such calls are initiated by police says something important about their predominant styles of working, it clearly does not constitute a perfect or complete substitution. Thus, the disposition of events in subsequent work, and the attendant refinement of the style measures that it would facilitate, is clearly called for. By the same token, despite the care with which they were selected for this study, the measures of neighborhood character that might pattern police work in a given area or, for that matter, in an entire city, are hardly exhausted by the set of indicators analyzed here. If local volatility is indeed worth examining, as the results presented in chapter 6 tend to hint, then measures of neighborhood change or its absence in critical indicators would add a notable sociohistorical dimension to a replicational exercise. So, for that matter, would the simple expansion of this work to include more cities in the United States, especially from regions west of the Mississippi River, and even cities from abroad as well.[3]

As noted earlier, this study is not the first to argue that police organizations are appropriate units of analysis, that their structures and dynamics are primary causal factors that determine how law enforcement will be carried out in the local community and how justice will be done and citizens served. To the contrary, this is in some ways an old argument, albeit one that has only rarely been tested in empirical research; it gains strength as empirical findings in support of it pile up from studies conducted in different settings, using different measurement tools and conventions. The findings from this effort are supportive of that argument as well. What they suggest, however, is nonetheless something a bit more. The police departments in our cities emerge from this study not simply as structural "black boxes" that produce results, but rather as *real* units of analysis: as entities that strive for, and to some degree achieve, the autonomy to plan and conduct action in a given social field, and to do so as entities. Sociologist James Coleman (1973) calls such units "corporate actors," and focuses much of his analysis on the ways in which they relate to individuals and the means by which they might be controlled. For the Elyria, Columbia, and Newark police departments, some aspects of the former have emerged from the neighborhood-level analyses of police action presented in chapter 6; for police organizations generally, a perspective on the latter will be offered in relatively short order. Before that, however, a prior question arises, one that highlights important research issues that could be fruitfully addressed in future efforts in the study of the police. That question can be stated, in admittedly anthropomorphic terms, generally as follows: if police agencies are really something akin to these corporate actors, how do

they go about "making up their minds" as to how they will act? How
do they decide what to do, as actors? How do they choose a style?

The first place to which this question directs attention is the police
organization itself. No formal organization is a perfectly meshed aggregate of individual working parts; to the contrary, individual members and formal units of larger organizations alternatively cooperate
and conflict with each other as they seek recognition and reward.
Police departments are no different in this regard from other formal
organizations; the two cultures of policing regularly come into conflict
over programmatic and operational policies and procedures. Nonetheless, police departments do manage, if our cities are any indication, to
deliver a definable, near-uniform product to almost all of the elements
of a diverse, differentiated "market." There must be a way—an organized process or at least a set of key elements—by means of which the
choice of style is communicated throughout the agency and its achieve-
ment in daily operations monitored. How is that accomplished? Muir
(1977) and Brown (1981) point to the important role of the sergeant in
this regard; Tifft (1975) generalizes a bit to focus on the unit supervisor of whatever rank. Case studies of innovations in policing demonstrate the power of supervisors to forestall and eventually destroy
operational experiments (Sherman et al. 1973); studies of nonpolice
organizations consistently turn up important operational effects traceable to the structure of supervisory ratios or administrative intensity.
The structure of supervision in the police organization is probably a
critical part of the answer to this question, but only further research
will provide the definitive statement in this regard. The question is
well worth addressing: how does the police command system process
the choice of a general departmental style, and how does it intervene
in the working out of that choice in daily police work? How does the
corporate actor in policing put its general policy decisions into operation consistently?

If this focus on police departments as corporate actors directs attention to matters of their internal structure and process, it also calls out
for a focus on questions of external relationships as well. Police agencies are not perfectly free actors; they are to at least a minimal degree formally and practically accountable to urban administrators and
policymakers. How do the forms that this accountability takes structure the corporate actor's decision? This, of course, is a straight-

forward extension of the question posed by Bordua and Reiss (1966) in their discussion of command, control, and charisma in policing and, as we have seen, the apparent answer is: quite significantly.

Nonetheless, Bordua and Reiss offer only a starting point for seeking a more complete answer to this question, for things are a good deal more complicated now than when they first offered their argument. Since 1966 we have seen the rise of police unions, the mounting of the professionalization movement in American policing and, most recently, large-scale racial transition in positions of power in big-city politics. All have effects on the style and the quality of local police service. Newark is a case in point; the battles that have raged in this city during the recent past between a popular elected black mayor, a respected professional police director, and a powerful, well-connected police union are ably described by Guyot (1983). For these and other reasons, the forging and reforging of police connections to urban administrators and political elites has become an inordinately complicated affair; to some observers, they make the contemporary city "ungovernable" (Yates 1977). All this has implications for the security of the police chief's tenure and the type of link between him or her and the urban executive—the two dimensions on which Bordua and Reiss built their original typology. Are new patterns of connection forged in this context between police and urban executives and, if so, how do these structure police style choices and command systems? In the face of such complications, are police executives increasingly thrown back on themselves and their organizations for making such choices and legitimating them? The latter is no less possible than the former, but in either event we need to know a good deal more than we do at present about the political constraints on our police corporate actor's policy options and choices.

When we envision any rational actor, corporate or otherwise, we usually conceive of one that evaluates and chooses among means in order to achieve one or more identifiable ends. The means-ends chain may be long, complex, and sophisticated, but it is nonetheless usually associated with our notions of the "rationality" of an actor. While the choice of a style made by a police corporate actor must clearly be a focus for future research, so too should be the evaluation process underlying such a choice. How do police organizations evaluate what they do in light of their overall choices of styles and how, as both citizens and researchers, should we? Identifying ways in which police departments might be made more efficient in expending their resources or by which they might make local citizens more satisfied with the service they deliver is an endeavor that deserves a distinctly secondary priority if the choice of a police organizational mission is not closely linked to such ends. Admittedly, no police department can afford for very long to squander funds and manpower outrageously, or to completely alienate the citizens with whom it comes into contact. However, once these floors of efficient use of resources and the satisfaction—or perhaps more accurately, indifference—of the citizens are attained, the question of evaluation opens up considerably, and the answer to it is by no means clear. How, for example, does one measure nonevents—absences of riots, disorders, or public displays of deviance—which are so avidly sought by the watchmanlike police agency? Against what performance standard, common and meaningful to both, can one compare a watchmanlike and a legalistic police department when the ends sought by each seem so different from one another? From the perspective of the police corporate actor, the answer might well be something like "maintenance of organizational freedom of action." In a democratic society, where normative theory demands governmental responsiveness to majority will as aggregated by and expressed through representative political institutions, that seems an insufficient and undemocratic answer, but the alternative is by no means clear.

All of these issues and questions that future police research might seek to tackle point ultimately to the larger topic of control of the police or, in somewhat more formal terms, to police accountability. James Coleman (1973) argues that the loss of power from individuals to corporate actors is large and irreversible without the construction of countervailing corporate actors. In the specific context of police, Michael Brown (1981) assesses four models of reform in order to achieve greater police accountability and suggests that all are seriously flawed, and that rather,

What is needed is a system of institutions which will permit continued reflection on the ends of police work and encourage responsiveness, while forcing the policeman to reexamine continually the contradiction between the ends he serves and the means he uses to attain them. (1981:304)

An institution that can permit, encourage, and force an outcome is a countervailing corporate actor in everything but name. To advocate its construction, of course, is to presume what future research should seek to establish: that the connections between police executives and urban policymakers are weak or even nonexistent, that police command systems do systematically transmit style choices across levels of the organization and monitor the results, and that the most powerful evaluative standard for police work to which police organizations actually pay attention is that of their own freedom of action. While we need not prejudge the results of future work, the perspective on police departments as rational corporate actors which emerges from the empirical findings presented here certainly points to accountability as an area for future study and experimentation.

The fact that accountability is worth such attention points to the final implication of the findings of this study and the perspective for which they argue. At the broadest level of generality, a perspective on police departments as organizational actors underscores the need for a reformulation of the model by which we think about the process of social control. As we have seen, standard models of control fare relatively poorly in our empirical analyses of police action, for police in Elyria, Columbia, and Newark do not invariably operate as simple agents of the resourceful in controlling the resourceless. As often as not in these cities, it is in the neighborhoods of the resourceful—those with stable families, high incomes, and relatively prestigious occupations—where police are aggressive enforcers of impartial law; as often as not, the resourceless are "treated with kid gloves" and are left alone unless they themselves summon the police. Unless it can be assumed (rather unreasonably, it would seem) that the neighborhoods of the resourceful in typical Elyria and thriving Columbia are so permeated with nonresident law violators as to constitute a crisis situation while the neighborhoods in declining, violent Newark are not, we must throw a severely critical glance at the standard model of police as agents of social control.

The problem with this standard model is in the area of "agency," for where a police department defines its own mission and the strategies by which to pursue it, it is to that extent no one's agent but its own. The general image of the police that most of us probably carry about is simply not designed to deal with a social control agent with a mind of its own, yet that apparently is what we face in the world of American policing.[4] Our models need rethinking and reworking.

In light of the explosion of police research that has recently occurred in American social science, and in light of the plethora of articles and books produced by that explosion, some might be tempted to ask: what remains to be done in research on the police? To the extent that we recognize American police agencies as rational actors, picking styles and mapping strategies around the constraints posed by diverse working environments, then the answer is indeed "quite a lot." The prospects for future work are rich and exciting.

Notes

1. Black (1976) offers an inventory of these in his attempt to build a behavioral theory of law in modern society. While the theory has been strongly criticized, the inventory itself is a thorough collection of the factors involved, and is worth attention in this regard.

2. Although he used data from surveys of police officers and conducted his research in metropolitan Los Angeles, Brown (1981) encountered virtually the identical result as that reported here with regard to the failure of variations in local crime rates to structure his empirical results on police officers' style orientations.

3. Shane (1980) makes limited use of similar dispatch data in a study of police work in nine cities distributed across five countries and, in doing so, demonstrates that much of the material they tap is or can easily be made comparable across research settings.

4. And, apparently, in other nations as well. Brogden (1982) paints a picture of the rise of police autonomy in recent years in England—specifically in Liverpool—that is in many ways parallel to the argument offered here.

References

Aberbach, Joel D. and J. L. Walker. 1970. "The Attitudes of Blacks and Whites Toward City Services: Implications for Public Policy." In John P. Crecine, ed. *Financing the Metropolis*, pp. 519–538. Beverly Hills: Sage.

Alex, Nicholas. 1969. *Black in Blue*. New York: Appleton-Century-Crofts.

Ames, Walter L. 1981. *Police and Community in Japan*. Berkeley: University of California Press.

Baker, Mary Holland, Barbara Nieustedt, Ronald S. Everett, and Richard McCleary. 1983. "Impact of a Crime Wave: Perceptions, Fear and Confidence in the Police." *Law and Society Review* 17:314–336.

Banton, Michael. 1964. *The Policeman in the Community*. New York: Basic.

Bayley, David H. 1969. *Police and Political Development in India*. Princeton: Princeton University Press.

——. 1976. *Forces of Order: Police Behavior in Japan and the United States*. Berkeley: University of California Press.

Bayley, David H. and Harold Mendelsohn. 1969. *Minorities and the Police*. New York: The Free Press.

Beirne, Piers. 1979. "Empiricism and the Critique of Marxism on Law and Crime." *Social Problems* 26:373–385.

Berk, Richard A. and Phyllis J. Newton. 1985. "Does Arrest Deter Wife Battery? An Effort to Replicate the Findings of the Minneapolis Spouse Abuse Experiment." *American Sociological Review* 50:253–262.

Berry, Brian J. L. 1972. "Latent Structure of the American Urban System, with International Comparisons." In Berry, ed. (1972):11–57.

Berry, Brian J. L., ed. 1972. *City Classification Handbook*. New York: Wiley.

——. 1976. *Urbanization and Counterurbanization*. Beverly Hills: Sage.

Berry, Brian J. L. and John D. Kasarda. 1977. *Contemporary Urban Ecology*. New York: Macmillan.

Bittner, Egon. 1967. "The Police on Skid Row: A Study of Peace Keeping." *American Sociological Review* 32:699–715.

Black, Donald. 1970. "The Production of Crime Rates." *American Sociological Review* 35:733–748.

——. 1976. *The Behavior of Law*. New York: Academic.

——. 1980. *The Manners and Customs of the Police*. New York: Academic.

Black, Donald and Albert J. Reiss Jr. 1970. "Police Control of Juveniles." *American Sociological Review* 35:63–77.

Blalock, Hubert M. 1982. *Conceptualization and Measurement in the Social Sciences.* Beverly Hills: Sage.

Blau, Peter M. 1963. *The Dynamics of Bureaucracy.* Chicago: University of Chicago Press.

———. 1972. "Interdependence and Hierarchy in Organizations." *Social Science Research* 1:1–24.

Blau, Peter M. and Richard A. Schoenherr. 1971. *The Structure of Organizations.* New York: Basic.

Bordua, David J. and Albert J. Reiss Jr. 1966. "Command, Control and Charisma: Reflections on Police Bureaucracy." *American Journal of Sociology* 72:68–76.

Bridenbaugh, Carl. 1938. *Cities in the Wilderness.* London: Oxford University Press.

———. 1955. *Cities in Revolt.* London: Oxford University Press.

Brogden, Michael. 1982. *The Police: Autonomy and Consent.* New York: Academic.

Brown, Michael K. 1981. *Working the Street: Police Discretion and the Dilemmas of Reform.* New York: Russell Sage Foundation.

Caiden, Gerald E. 1977. *Police Revitalization.* Lexington: D. C. Heath.

Clark, Terry Nichols. 1968. "Community Structure, Decision-Making, Budget Expenditures, and Urban Renewal in 51 American Communities." *American Sociological Review* 33:576–593.

Clark, Terry N. 1973. *Community Power and Policy Outputs.* Beverly Hills: Sage.

Clark, Terry Nichols and Lorna Crowley Ferguson. 1983. *City Money.* New York: Columbia University Press.

Coleman, James S. 1973. "Loss of Power." *American Sociological Review* 38:1–17.

———. 1974. *Power and the Structure of Society.* New York: W. W. Norton.

———. 1982. *The Assymetric Society.* Syracuse: Syracuse University Press.

Collins, Randall. 1975. *Conflict Sociology: Toward an Explanatory Science.* New York: Academic.

Davis, Kenneth Culp. 1975. *Police Discretion.* St. Paul: West.

Downes, Bryan T. 1968. "Social and Political Characteristics of Riot Cities: A Comparative Study." *Social Science Quarterly* 49:504–520.

Ericson, Richard V. 1982. *Reproducing Order: A Study of Police Patrol Work.* Toronto: University of Toronto Press.

Ferdinand, Thomas N. 1976. "From a Service to a Legalistic Style Department: A Case Study." *Journal of Police Science and Administration* 4:302–319.

Fischer, Claude S. 1972. "Urbanism As a Way of Life: A Review and An Agenda." *Sociological Methods and Research* 1:187–242.

———. 1981. *To Dwell Among Friends: Personal Networks in Towns and City.* Chicago: University of Chicago Press.

Fishman, Mark. 1978. "Crime Waves as Ideology." *Social Problems* 25:531–543.

Fogelson, Robert M. 1977. *Big-City Police*. Cambridge: Harvard University Press.

Freeman, John and Michael T. Hannan. 1983. "Niche Width and the Dynamics of Organization Populations." *American Journal of Sociology* 88:1116–1145.

Galle, O. R., W. R. Gove and J. M. McPherson. 1972. "Population Density and Pathology: What Are the Relationships For Man?" *Science* 176:23–30.

Gans, Herbert J. 1962. *The Urban Villagers: Group and Class in the Life of Italian-Americans*. Glencoe: The Free Press.

Gibbs, Jack P. 1982. "Law as a Means of Social Control." Jack P. Gibbs, ed. *Social Control: Views from the Social Sciences*, pp. 83–114. Beverly Hills: Sage.

Gould, Stephen Jay. 1981. *The Mismeasure of Man*. New York: Norton.

Greisinger, George W., Jeffrey S. Slovak, and Joseph J. Molkup. 1979. *Civil Service Systems: Their Impact on Police Administration*. Washington, D.C.: GPO.

Guyot, Dorothy. 1983. "Newark: Crime and Politics in a Declining City." In Heinz, Jacob, and Lineberry, eds. (1983). pp. 23–96. New York: Longmans.

Hage, Jerald. 1980. *Theories of Organization*. New York: Academic.

Hannan, Michael T. and John Freeman. 1984. "Structural Inertia and Organizational Change." *American Sociological Review* 49:149–164.

Harman, Harry. 1976. *Modern Factor Analysis*. Chicago: University of Chicago Press.

Harris, Richard N. 1973. *The Police Academy: An Inside View*. New York: Wiley.

Hawley, Amos H. 1950. *Human Ecology: A Theory of Community Structure*. New York: Ronald Press.

———. 1971. *Urban Society: An Ecological Approach*. New York: Ronald Press.

Hawley, Willis D. 1975. *Non-Partisan Elections and the Case for Party Politics*. New York: Wiley.

Hays, Samuel P. 1964. "The Politics of Reform in Municipal Government in the Progressive Era." *Pacific Northwest Quarterly* 55:159–169.

Heinz, Anne, Herbert Jacob, and Robert L. Lineberry, eds. 1983. *Crime in City Politics*. New York: Longmans.

Hirschman, Albert O. 1970. *Exit, Voice and Loyalty: Responses to Decline in Firms, Organizations and States*. Cambridge: Harvard University Press.

Hodson, Randy and Robert L. Kaufmann. 1982. "Economic Dualism: A Critical Review." *American Sociological Review* 47:727–739.

Hofstadter, Richard. 1955. *The Age of Reform*. New York: Vintage.

Hunter, Albert. 1974. *Symbolic Communities: The Persistence and Change of Chicago's Local Communities*. Chicago: University of Chicago Press.

Jackson, Pamela Irving and Leo Carroll. 1981. "Race and the War on Crime." *American Sociological Review* 46:290–305.

Jacob, Herbert and Michael J. Rich. 1981. "The Effects of the Police on Crime: A Second Look." *Law and Society Review* 15:109–122.

Jacobs, David. 1979. "Inequality and Police Strength." *American Sociological Review* 44:913–924.

Janowitz, Morris. 1969. *Institution-Building in Urban Education.* Chicago: University of Chicago Press.

——. 1976. *Social Control of the Welfare State.* Chicago: University of Chicago Press.

Janson, Carl-Gunnar. 1968. "The Spatial Structure of Newark, New Jersey. Part I: The Central City." *Acta Sociologica* 2:144–169.

Kansas City, Missouri, Police Department. 1977. *Response Time Analysis: Executive Summary.* Kansas City: Board of Police Commissioners.

Kasarda, John D. 1972. "The Impact of Suburban Population Growth on Central City Service Functions." *American Journal of Sociology* 77:1111–1124.

Kelling, George F. 1983. "On the Accomplishments of the Police." Maurice Punch, ed. (1983):152–164.

Kelling, George L., Tony Pate, Duane Dieckman and Charles E. Brown. 1974. *The Kansas City Preventive Patrol Experiment: Summary Report.* Washington, D.C.: Police Foundation.

Knoke, David. 1982. "The Spread of Municipal Reform: Temporal, Spatial and Social Dynamics." *American Journal of Sociology* 87:1314–1339.

LaFave, Wayne R. 1965. *Arrest: The Decision to Take a Suspect Into Custody.* Boston: Little, Brown.

Lane, Roger. 1967. *Policing the City: Boston 1822–1885.* Cambridge: Harvard University Press.

Larsen, Richard C. 1972. *Urban Police Patrol Analysis.* Cambridge: MIT Press.

Lawrence, Paul R. and Jay W. Lorsch. 1967. *Environment and Organization.* Cambridge: Harvard University Press.

Leinen, Stephen. 1984. *Black Police, White Society.* New York: New York University Press.

Liang, Hsi-Huey. 1970. *The Berlin Police Force in the Weimar Republic.* Berkeley: University of California Press.

Lipsky, Machael. 1980. *Street-Level Bureaucracy: Dilemmas of the Individual in Public Services.* New York: Russell Sage Foundation.

Liska, Allen E. and Mitchell B. Chamlin. 1984. "Social Structure and Crime Control among Macrostructural Units." *American Journal of Sociology* 90:383–395.

Liska, Allen E., Joseph J. Lawrence, and Michael Benson. 1981. "Perspectives on the Legal Order: The Capacity for Social Control." *American Journal of Sociology* 87:413–426.

Loftin, Colin and David McDowall. 1982. "The Police, Crime and Economic Theory." *American Sociological Review* 47:393–401.

Loftin, Colin, Ronald C. Kessler, and David F. Greenberg. 1984. "Social Inequality and Crime Control." Presented at the annual meeting of the American Society of Criminology.

Manning, Peter K. 1974. "Police Lying." *Urban Life and Culture* 3:283–306.

——. 1983. "Organizational Control and Semiotics." In Punch, ed. (1983): 169–193.

————. 1977. *Police Work: The Social Organization of Policing.* Cambridge: MIT Press.

————. 1978a. "Rules, Colleagues and Situationally Justified Actions." In Manning and John Van Maanen, eds. (1978):71–90.

————. 1978b. "Lying, Secrecy and Social Control." In Manning and Van Maanen, eds. (1978):238–254.

Manning, Peter K. and John Van Maanen, eds. 1978. *Policing: A View from the Street.* Santa Monica: Goodyear.

Martin, Susan Ehrlich. 1980. *Breaking and Entering: Policewomen on Patrol.* Berkeley: University of California Press.

Milton, Catherine H. 1972. *Women in Policing.* Washington, D.C.: The Police Foundation.

Mintzberg, Henry. 1973. *The Nature of Managerial Work.* New York: Harper and Row.

Muir, William Ker Jr. 1977. *Police: Streetcorner Politicians.* Chicago: University of Chicago Press.

Niederhoffer, Arthur. 1969. *Behind the Shield: The Police in Urban Society.* Garden City: Anchor.

Ostrom, Elinor, William H. Baugh, Richard Guaraschi, Roger B. Parks, and Gordon P. Whitaker. 1973. "Community Organization and the Provision of Police Services." Beverly Hills: Sage: Administrative and Policy Series No. 03-001.

Ostrom, Elinor and Roger B. Parks. 1973. "Suburban Police Departments: Too Many and Too Small?" In Louis Masotti and Jeffrey Hadden, eds. *The Urbanization of the Suburbs.* Beverly Hills: Sage.

Parks, Roger B. and Elinor Ostrom. 1981. "Complex Models of Urban Service Systems." Pp. 171–199 in Terry Nichols Clark, ed. *Urban Policy Analysis: Directions for Future Research.* Beverly Hills: Sage.

Pfeffer, Jeffrey and Gerald R. Salancik. 1978. *The External Control of Organizations: A Resource-Dependence Perspective.* New York: Harper and Row.

Phillips, Charles D. and Alissa Politzer. 1982. "Effects of Police Action on Perceived Victimization." Presented at the annual meeting of the Law and Society Association, Toronto, Canada.

Piliavin, Irving M. and Scott Briar. 1964. "Police Encounters With Juveniles." *American Journal of Sociology* 70:206–214.

Pondy, Louis R. 1969. "Effects of Size, Complexity and Ownership on Administrative Intensity." *Administrative Science Quarterly* 14:47–60.

Prottas, Jeffrey Manditch. 1978. "The Power of the Street-Level Bureaucrat in Public Service Bureaucracies." *Urban Affairs Quarterly* 14:285–312.

Punch, Maurice, ed. 1983. *Control in the Police Organization.* Cambridge: MIT Press.

Rees, Philip H. 1972. "Problems of Classifying Subareas Within Cities." In Berry, ed. (1972):265–330.

Reiss, Albert J. Jr. and David J. Bordua. 1967. "Environment and Organization: A Perspective on Police." In David J. Bordua, ed. *The Police: Six Sociological Essays,* pp. 25–55. New York: Wiley.

Reuss-Ianni, Elizabeth. 1983. *The Two Cultures of Policing: Street Cops and Management Cops*. New Brunswick: Transaction Books.

Reuss-Ianni, Elizabeth and Francis A. J. Ianni. 1983. "Street Cops and Management Cops: The Two Cultures of Policing." In Punch, ed. (1983):251–274.

Richardson, James F. 1970. *The New York Police: Colonial Times to 1901*. Cambridge: Harvard University Press.

Robinson, William S. 1950. "Ecological Correlation and the Behavior of Individuals." *American Sociological Review* 15:351–357.

Rossi, Peter H. and Robert L. Crain. 1968. "The NORC Permanent Community Sample." *Public Opinion Quarterly* 32:261–272.

Rossi, Peter H., Richard A. Berk, and Bettye K. Eidson. 1974. *The Roots of Urban Discontent*. New York: Wiley.

Rubinstein, Jonathan. 1973. *City Police*. New York: Farrar, Straus and Giroux.

Rushing, William A. 1967. "The Effects of Industry Size and Division of Labor on Administration." *Administrative Science Quarterly* 12:273–295.

Schnore, Leo F. and Robert R. Alford. 1963. "Forms of Government and Socioeconomic Characteristics of Suburbs." *Administrative Science Quarterly* 8:1–17.

Shane, Paul G. 1980. *Police and People: A Comparison of Five Countries*. New York: Mosby.

Sherman, Lawrence W. et al. 1973. *Team Policing: Seven Case Studies*. Washington, D.C.: The Police Foundation.

Sherman, Lawrence W. and Richard A. Berk. 1984. "The Specific Deterrent Effects of Arrest for Domestic Assault." *American Sociological Review* 49:261–272.

Simmel, Georg. 1903. "The Metropolis and Mental Life." In Paul K. Hatt and Albert J. Reiss Jr. eds. *Cities and Society*, pp. 635–646. Glencoe: The Free Press: 1957.

Skogan, Wesley G. 1976. "Efficiency and Effectiveness in Big-City Police Departments." *Public Administration Review* 36:278–286.

Skolnick, Jerome K. 1967. *Justice Without Trial: Law Enforcement in Democratic Society*. New York: Wiley.

Slovak, Jeffrey S. 1978. "Work Satisfaction and Municipal Police Officers." *Journal of Police Science and Administration* 6:78–87.

———. 1983. "Violence in the City: Empirical Bases for a Collective Working Image." *Journal of Criminal Justice* 11:301–316.

———. 1985. "City Spending, Suburban Demands and Fiscal Exploitation: A Replication and Extension." *Social Forces* 64:168–190.

Smith, Michael P. 1979. *The City and Social Theory*. New York: St. Martins.

Suttles, Gerald D. 1968. *The Social Order of the Slum: Ethnicity and Territory in the Inner City*. Chicago: University of Chicago Press.

Sykes, Richard E. and Edward E. Brent. 1983. *Policing: A Social Behaviorst Perspective*. New Brunswick: Rutgers University Press.

Sykes, Richard E. and John P. Clark. 1975. "A Theory of Deference Exchange in Police-Civilian Encounters." *American Journal of Sociology* 81:584–600.

Talarico, Susette M. and Charles R. Swanson Jr. 1978. "Styles of Policing: A Preliminary Mapping." *Policy Studies Journal* 7:398–406.

Tifft, Larry L. 1975. "Control Systems, Social Bases of Power and Power Exercise in Police Organizations." *Journal of Police Science and Administration* 3:66–76.

Timms, Duncan. 1971. *The Urban Mosaic: Towards a Theory of Residential Differentiation*. Cambridge: Cambridge University Press.

U.S. Department of Justice. 1976. *Criminal Victimization Surveys in Eight Individual Cities: A Comparison of 1972 and 1975 Findings*. Washington, D.C.: GPO.

Van Maanen, John. 1975. "Police Socialization: A Longitudinal Examination of Job Attitudes in an Urban Police Department." *Administrative Science Quarterly* 20:207–228.

Votey, H. L. and L. Phillips. 1972. "Police Effectiveness and the Production Function for Law Enforcement." *Journal of Legal Studies* 1:1–15.

Weber, Max. 1922. *The Theory of Social and Economic Organization*. Talcott Parsons, trans. New York: The Free Press: 1964.

Westley, William A. 1953. "Violence and the Police." *American Journal of Sociology* 59:34–41.

———. 1956. "Secrecy and the Police." *Social Forces* 34:254–257.

———. 1970. *Violence and the Police: A Sociological Study of Law, Custom and Morality*. Cambridge: MIT Press.

Williams, Alan. 1979. *The Police of Paris, 1718–1789*. Baton Rouge: Louisiana State University Press.

Wilson, James Q. 1972. *Varieties of Police Behavior: The Management of Law and Order in Eight Communities*. New York: Atheneum. (Note: this book was originally published in 1968 by Harvard University Press.)

Wilson, James Q. and Barbara Boland. 1978. "The Effect of the Police on Crime." *Law and Society Review* 12:367–390.

Wirth, Louis. 1938. "Urbanism as a Way of Life." *American Journal of Sociology* 44:3–24.

Yates, Douglas. 1977. *The Ungovernable City: The Politics of Urban Problems and Policy-Making*. Cambridge: MIT Press.

Zerubavel, Eviatar. 1981. *Hidden Rhythms: Schedules and Calendars in Social Life*. Chicago: University of Chicago Press.

Index

198   *Index*